The Knitter's Curiosity Cabinet

Hunter Hammersen

The Knitter's Curiosity Cabinet

20 Patterns Inspired by Vintage Botanical Illustrations

Hunter Hammersen

Pantsville Press

Photography by Making the Moment LLC

Book design and cover design by Zoë Lonergan

Charts created with StitchMastery Knitting Chart Editor

ISBN: 978-0-9849982-0-3

Library of Congress Control Number: 2011946276

First Printing, 2012
Printed in China with Asia Pacific Offset

Pantsville Press
Cleveland, Ohio
www.pantsvillepress.com

CONTENTS

For Peter.

I so wish I could have shown this to you.
Oh and that reminds me of the time...

ACKNOWLEDGEMENTS

I used to think that writing a book was a solitary task. I had an image of an author, sitting in a studio (bonus points if it overlooked some dramatic lonely landscape), typing away, accompanied by no one but a cat. It seems it doesn't work that way. At least not for me. My books are more of a group affair. As such, I've accumulated a long list of debts.

One of the largest of these is that owed to my test and sample knitters. They generously lent me their time and skill and were a source of tremendous support and encouragement. They have done me (and everyone who uses this book) an invaluable service. They are Elizabeth Inman, Kristina Bird, Jody Strine, Joanna Waldstreicher, Elizabeth Rislove Etler, Nicole Kent, Jeri Mihm, Antonia Markiet, Jise Brackbill, Jessica Powers, Barb Stephenson, Ellen Stratton, Christy Herbert, Beth Loft, Shannon Pucek, Audrey Tam, and Angela Grob.

Many thanks are also due to my lovely friends, Lauren Falk, Stacey Kolthammer, and Jennifer Williams for spending a slightly surreal fall day striking poses. Their enthusiasm and spirit shine in every picture. Brett Yacovella and his assistant Renee Dunn kept us smiling all day long, and Elle Gemma helped everyone look their best. James Edmonson, Jennifer Nieves, and Laura Travis of the Dittrick Medical History Center and Dzwinka Holian of the Allen Memorial Medical Library were kind enough to let us invade their amazing facilities for the day. I couldn't have asked for a better location.

I can't possibly say enough nice things about Cathy Scott. She's the genius behind the software used to make the charts shown in this book. Just creating that software would have put all of us in her debt, but she was also kind enough to make all of the charts used here. She and Lorna Wilkey both served as the most gracious tech editors imaginable. They pointed out my foolish mistakes so you don't have to. If your knitting goes smoothly, it is in large part due to their diligence and attention to detail (and if it doesn't, it's undoubtedly because I failed to listen to them).

I owe a similar debt of gratitude to Heather Ordover, Sonia Verma, and Lana Holden. They were all brave enough to look at the early drafts of this book (a daunting prospect if ever there was one) and provided no end of helpful suggestions and tactful corrections. The ever-charming Zoë Lonergan faced her own challenging task. She skilfully transformed my vague ideas, jotted notes, and jumble of files into a book that is both lovely and easy to use, a feat for which I will be forever grateful.

I would be remiss were I not to mention Cat Bordhi and her Visionary Authors program. Cat's support and encouragement of independent designers is changing the industry and making it a much more exciting time to be a knitter. She has created an amazing community, and I am honored to be a part of it.

And of course, I have to thank my family. They've taken this new obsession of mine in complete stride. It isn't quite what I thought I'd do when I was a kid (apparently I wanted to be both a ballerina and fence painter at one point), and it's not what I went to school for (those engineering classes don't come in handy too often, but the history ones certainly seem to have made an impression), but it seems to be working out. And last but never least, uncountable thanks to my husband Brian. He hears all my ideas when they are fragile, newborn things, and he is always gentle with them. This book, and any that come after it, are here because of his unflagging support.

INTRODUCTION

There are rocks in the trunk of my car right now—probably a few sticks too. The odd seashell or pinecone isn't out of the question either. And it doesn't stop with my car. My husband's car falls prey to my magpie tendencies too, as does any suitcase that accompanies me on a trip. This isn't a new development. I've been picking up pebbles and arrowheads and fossils and whatever else catches my eye for as long as I can remember. So perhaps it's no surprise that when I first learned of curiosity cabinets, I felt an instant spark of recognition and understanding. Apparently I'm not the only one fascinated by the array of things the world has to offer (nor the only one subject to a bit of a collecting urge). It turns out there's a long history of assembling collections of personal treasures. I'm in good company.

A little while ago, the idea of a knitter's curiosity cabinet took hold of my imagination and simply refused to let go. The thought of assembling a collection, not of rocks and seeds and fossils, but of fancy edgings and captivating stitch patterns and fabulous shapes was too good to ignore. This book is the result. Each of the patterns was inspired by (and named after) a vintage botanical illustration. Illustrations were one of the ways people documented and shared the contents of their curiosity cabinets. I designed two patterns from each of the prints: one for a pair of socks and one for something else entirely. Each project offers something special that I hope will catch your eye and inspire you to add it to your own collection.

HISTORY

The word *science* conjures up visions of gleaming laboratories filled with sophisticated equipment and powerful computers. Science has mapped the genome, split the atom, and ventured into the heavens. It seems an utterly modern enterprise. It's easy to forget that science as we think of it today is a relatively recent development. Science has its roots in incantations and potions and alchemy. The path from there to here was long and complicated, and curiosity cabinets had an important part to play in the transition.

Ideas rarely spring fully formed from the ether. They grow and evolve, sometimes directly and sometimes in an unabashedly circuitous fashion, from a variety of predecessors. Curiosity cabinets and the ideas they embody are no exceptions. With a little imagination, you could trace the impulse behind them to the earliest days of human history when ancient people carefully collected matching snail shells to make ornaments, or to ancient Egypt when artisans sought out colorful gemstones to shape into jewelry, or to the early days of the Christian church when the pious assembled collections of relics to venerate. But their more direct history begins in western Europe starting around 1500.

The 1500s were a period of great exploration. Europeans were discovering the wonders of the New World and at the same time rediscovering the knowledge of the ancient world. People were struggling to make sense of their rapidly expanding universe, and assembling curiosity cabinets was one of the ways they did it.

People at the highest levels of society—kings and cardinals, popes and princes—assembled curiosity cabinets to both display the new wonders the world had to offer and show off their own power and prestige. At this point, the word *cabinet* didn't always refer to a standalone piece of furniture. It could also be used for a chamber or a room. These rooms varied in size and scale, but they were usually lined with cupboards that held an astonishing array of treasures. Items from the natural world (plants, fossils, shells, minerals, skeletons) sat side by side with man-made objects (paintings, statues, coins, models, tools). The contents were eclectic in the extreme, and they often included items of dubious authenticity such as unicorn horns or remnants of sea monsters. Many of these earliest cabinets were intensely personal spaces intended only for the enjoyment of their owners. Prized possessions were kept hidden safely away behind locked doors, and only the collection's owner knew where to find them. These were private treasure troves intended for contemplation and solitary enjoyment. They might occasionally be shared with family or with people you sought to impress, but they were not open to scholars, and certainly not to the general public. Even if scholars were to gain admittance, the contents were so haphazardly acquired and assembled that they were unlikely to prove of much use. But these rather eccentric princely cabinets were soon augmented by more focused scholarly collections.

By the late 1500s, ideas about how knowledge of the world should be obtained and used were changing. The Aristotelian world view in which the Earth sits solidly at the center of the universe and all matter is made of some combination of earth, air, water, and fire had held sway for hundreds of years. But it was now beginning to be challenged. It was becoming ever less acceptable to sit and philosophize about how the universe or the world ought to work. Some people now thought it much better to observe the world directly and draw conclusions from those observations. Curiosity cabinets, with their collections of natural wonders, aided in this observation. Francis Bacon, writing in 1594 on how to increase and encourage knowledge of the world, suggested amassing "a goodly huge cabinet, wherein ... whatsoever singularity, chance, and the shuffle of things hath produced; whatsoever nature hath wrought ... shall be sorted and included." By so doing, you could create "a model of universal nature made private."

The scholarly cabinets assembled in the 1600s reflected this new approach. Indiscriminate acquisition for the sake of demonstrating power and scope of influence became less popular. More focused and specific collections became the order of the day. Objects were brought together because they could be used to analyze the world and to better understand how it worked. Collections were carefully vetted, and great care was taken to arrange items logically and store them in an accessible way. It was now important to be able to find specific specimens, not just to present an impressive display. Curiosity cabinets became a sort of laboratory where scholars sought to engage with and understand the natural world. This style of hands-on observation and interaction became central to how new knowledge was created. Richard Fortey put it beautifully when he explained that "collections provide the ground ... on which hypotheses are built." At the same time, as printing technology improved and it became practical to reproduce highly detailed images, catalogs of collections became popular and allowed an ever-increasing number of scholars to explore the contents of various cabinets.

Frontispiece from Museum Wormianum, a catalog of the contents of Ole Worm's collection published after his death in 1655. Note the large proportion of natural (as opposed to man-made) items and the careful categorization of the collection.

Just as curiosity cabinets became an important tool for scholars, they also became popular with ordinary citizens. Personal cabinets could range from the extensive and undeniably grand to the far more humble. An impressive cabinet was something to be proud of and was a symbol of social standing. Many doctors and apothecaries assembled substantial collections to demonstrate their command of the natural world. But private collections didn't always have a specific focus. Many were almost as eclectic as the princely cabinets that came before them. But unlike their

Standalone cabinet made for Sweden's King Gustavus Adolphus. The cabinet was created in Augsburg between 1625 and 1631 by Philipp Hainhofer. Note the wide variety of objects both man-made and natural. Image courtesy of the Uppsala University Art Collections. All rights reserved.

predecessors, personal cabinets were intended to be shared. They were fundamentally social creations. They were displayed, either in places of business or in the public areas of homes, and were intended as conversation pieces.

And so, by the 1700s, the princely cabinets of the 1500s, intended as a private display of power, had given way to two new forms: the scholarly cabinet and the personal cabinet. Both new forms were far more public, and both were ways of exploring the world rather than of expressing dominion over it. The contents of many scholarly cabinets went on to serve as the foundation for some

of the earliest natural history museums while the spirit behind personal cabinets still resonates with collectors and artists today.

Painting of an eclectic personal cabinet. Note the small scale, modest housing, and wide assortment of items. Painted by Domenico Remps, likely in the 1690s. Image courtesy of the Museo dell'Opificio Delle Pietre Dure, Florence. All rights reserved.

PRINTS

There is a long tradition of making exquisitely detailed catalogs of the items in curiosity cabinets. Preparing these catalogs was a costly and complicated undertaking. Commissioning illustrations and overseeing printing involved substantial outlays of both time and money. But it became increasingly common and served several purposes.

Since it was almost never possible to complete a collection (collectors are rarely sated), an illustration of an item held by a fellow collector could serve as a placeholder and fill in the gaps in another collection. Illustrations also captured aspects of items that were difficult to preserve. Plant and animal specimens degraded over time while pictures remained vibrant. Perhaps most importantly, as interest in the subject grew, published catalogs of cabinets made their contents accessible to people who could never hope to visit them in person.

I would have loved to work with images from some of these early catalogs. They were small works of art. They were also costly and usually published in very small numbers. The intervening years have made them both rarer and more expensive. The few originals I could find for sale were well out of my price range. Just as important, not all of them lent themselves to being adapted as knitting patterns. I could have worked from reproductions. Several of the catalogs have been reproduced in modern editions, and many of the others are available in digital versions. But I wanted to work from the originals, from something I could hold in my hands.

The joy of collecting is a fundamental part of the appeal of curiosity cabinets, and I admit that a bit of this collector's impulse influenced my desire to actually own the images I used in the book. So I turned to a slightly more available resource, prints from works of natural history. These were very much inspired by the same spirit of exploration and classification that lay behind curiosity cabinets,

but tended to be printed in larger numbers. They also included even more specimens. This meant that I had a wider array of images to choose from and that I could afford to indulge my desire to own the pieces I worked with. I hope you will forgive me this small lapse.

Rubus suberectus is from *English Botany or Coloured Figures of British Plants with their Essential Characters, Synonyms, and Places of Growth*. This was written by James Edward Smith and illustrated by James Sowerby. It was released as a series of 36 volumes between 1790 and 1813. It is a massive collection featuring more than than 2,500 plants.

Crocus vernus and *Narcissus pseudo-narcissus* are from *Flora von Deutschland*. This impressive work shows over 3,000 plants. It was originally compiled by Diederich Schlechtendal, Christian Langethal, and Ernst Schenk in the 1840s as a 24-volume edition. It was revised in the 1880s and republished as part of a 30-volume set edited by Ernst Hallier. These images come from that later edition.

Chrysanthemum frutescens, *Loasa lateritia*, and *Linaria bipartita* are from *Favourite Flowers of Garden and Greenhouse*, a four-volume collection assembled by Edward Step and William Watson. The volumes were published in 1896 and 1897 and describe more than 300 of the most popular English garden plants. The books were meant for a general (rather than a scientific) audience and provided both pictures of the plants and tips for their care.

Pinus silvestris, *Polypodium vulgare*, *Dianthus superbus*, and *Rosa rubiginosa* are from *Bilder ur Nordens Flora*. This three-volume work includes more than 650 plants and was written by the Swedish botanist Carl Lindman and published between 1901 and 1905.

TIPS

This book doesn't teach you how to knit. I assume you already know the basics (how to knit and purl, how to increase and decrease, and how to work flat and in the round). If you've got those things down, you can make any of these projects.

That said, there are a few little things that might be useful to know ahead of time. Most of these are fairly standard knitting pattern conventions, so if you want to skip ahead to the patterns, please feel free. But if you happen find yourself with a question, you might want to come back here and see if some of this information helps. Topics are organized in alphabetical order to help you quickly find exactly what you're looking for.

Abbreviations: See the stitch key for a complete list of all the abbreviations used in the text of the patterns.

Cast on: Use any stretchy cast on you like. All of the projects shown in the pictures were made with the long-tailed cast on or a provisional cast on. If you have a personal favorite, feel free to use it instead.

Cast off: Use any stretchy cast off you like. Jeny's Surprisingly Stretchy Bind Off, as described in the Fall 2009 issue of *Knitty*, is a good choice for most projects.

Charts: All of these patterns use at least one chart. Charts are easy to work with, but they do require a bit of attention if you've not used them before. The important thing to remember is that charts show you a stylized picture of what the right side of your knitting will look like.

If you're working in the round, the right side of your fabric is always facing you, so the chart always shows you exactly what to do. Just read each row of the chart from right to left and make the stitch indicated in the right-side instructions in the stitch key.

If you're working back and forth, the procedure is a bit different. When you're working a right-side row, read that row of the chart from right to left and make the stitch indicated in the right-side instructions in the stitch key. When you're working a wrong-side row, read that row of the chart from left to right and make the stitch indicated in the wrong-side instructions in the stitch key.

Chart notes: Some of the charts include notes to draw your attention to particular features or help you with potential trouble spots. Please be sure to read these notes carefully before you begin.

Gauge: Adjusting your gauge is one of the easiest ways to fine tune the size of your finished object. This can be a bit risky if you're making something closely fitted like a sweater (it works, you just need to do a fair bit of planning and some math). But it's a perfectly reasonable approach for most of the projects in this book. Though if you try it, it is helpful to keep a few things in mind.

First, always remember that the finished size of a particular bit of knitting at any given spot is is going to be (more or less) the total number of stitches at that spot divided by the gauge. So if you've cast on 72 stitches for a sock, and you're getting a gauge of 9 stitches per inch, you divide 72 stitches by 9 stitches per inch to get size of 8 inches. For this to work, it's important that you're measuring your gauge over the stitch pattern you're using and over a blocked swatch (if you're going to block the finished object). This is a very handy bit of math and it gives you a tremendous amount of flexibility in substituting yarns or in adjusting the size of a finished object.

Second, adjusting the gauge of your socks requires a bit more thought than adjusting the gauge of your shawl or your cowl. Socks have to deal with some rather demanding conditions. The single best thing you can do to ensure the longevity of your socks is knit tightly enough that you get a firm fabric *in your chosen yarn*. That means if you've picked a thin sock yarn, you may need to knit at 9 or 9.5 stitches per inch. By the same token, if you've picked a thick sock yarn, you may be able to knit at 7.5 or 7 stitches per inch.

If you've selected a yarn that works best at a gauge different from that listed in the pattern, you should do a bit of math to figure out which of the sizes will work best for you. The easiest way to understand this is with an example. Say you've decided to make the *Linaria bipartita* socks, and that your foot is about 8.5 inches around. This sock comes in three sizes (56, 64, and 72 stitches), and it calls for a gauge of 8 stitches per inch.

If you're using a yarn that gives you a good sock fabric at 8 stitches per inch, you should make the 64-stitch size (64 stitches divided by 8 stitches per inch gives an 8-inch sock, which will fit an 8.5-inch foot).

If you're using a yarn that gives you a good sock fabric at 7 stitches per inch, the 64-stitch size won't work (64 stitches divided by 7 stitches per inch gives a sock a little over 9 inches, which would be too big). Instead, you need to make the 56-stitch size (56 stitches divided by 7 stitches per inch gives an 8-inch sock, which will fit an 8.5-inch foot).

If you're using a yarn that gives you a good sock fabric at 9 stitches per inch, the 64-stitch size won't work (64 stitches divided by 9 stitches per inch gives a sock a little over 7 inches around, which would be too small). Instead you need to make the 72-stitch size (72 stitches divided by 9 stitches per inch gives an 8-inch sock, which will fit an 8.5-inch foot).

The general guideline is, if you've chosen a *thicker* yarn and are getting *fewer* stitches per inch than what the pattern calls for, consider making a smaller size. If you've chosen a *thinner* yarn and are getting *more* stitches per inch than what the pattern calls for, consider making a larger size. But you should always double check the math to make sure that it will work for you.

Grafting: Graft the ends of your toes however you like. All of the projects shown in the pictures were grafted with kitchener stitch.

Heel flaps: Heel flaps are worked back and forth over somewhere around half of the stitches of the sock. Each sock pattern lists the specific stitches that are to be used for the heel flap. Be sure to read carefully to see which stitches to use.

It is easy to adjust the height of your heel flap to make your sock really fit your foot. To figure out the right height, try slipping a rubber band around your ankle, standing up, and rolling it as far down as it will go. Make sure it's straight and measure from the bottom of the rubber band to the floor. Try making your heel flap just a bit shorter than that measurement. Just be sure to work an even number of rows so you're lined up properly to continue with the heel turn.

Pattern repeats: Generally, a chart shows one full repeat of a stitch pattern. Unless otherwise noted, this stitch pattern is worked across or around the entire row or round of the piece.

For example, the Main Chart for the *Loasa lateritia* sock is 8 stitches wide. The sock itself is 56, 64, or 72 stitches around, depending on the size you're making. When the pattern tells you to "work the Main Chart once," that means repeat the 8 stitches of row 1 of the Main Chart 7, 8, or 9 times to use up all 56, 64, or 72 stitches of the round. Then repeat the 8 stitches of row 2 of the Main Chart 7, 8, or 9 times to use up all 56, 64, or 72 stitches of the round. Continue in this fashion until all rows have been worked.

Put another way, "work the chart" means repeat the stitches of the chart over and over across the entire row or round until you reach the end.

Needles: All the patterns are written to work with any style of needle. You can use double points, one circular, two circulars, or anything else you can come up with, and you can arrange your stitches across your needles however you like. The only thing to keep in mind is that you will occasionally be told to work on certain stitches while setting others aside (for example when you make a heel flap). When this happens, just count from the beginning of the row or round to find the required stitches and rearrange as needed.

Notes: Several of the patterns include special notes. These are intended to draw your attention to important aspects of the patterns. Please be sure to read these notes carefully before you begin.

Right side: The right side of your knitting is the outside or the public side. It is abbreviated RS throughout the text.

Shaded stitches: Some charts use shading to draw your attention to certain stitches. When this happens, there will always be a note explaining the specific instructions for that particular pattern. Please be sure to read these notes carefully before you begin.

Sizing: Each of the patterns is offered in at least two sizes. Sometimes stitch counts or pattern repeats or other instructions differ from one size to the next. This is indicated by first giving the stitch count or pattern repeat for the smallest size and then giving the stitch count or pattern repeat for the larger sizes in square brackets. If there is more than one larger size, the stitch counts or pattern repeats will be separated by commas. So the instruction "Cast on 24 [36, 48] stitches" means cast on 24 stitches if you are making the smallest size, cast on 36 stitches if you are making the medium size, and cast on 48 stitches if you are making the largest size.

Sometimes sizing is indicated on the charts by shading certain squares. When this happens, there will always be a note explaining the specific instructions for that particular pattern. Please be sure to read these notes carefully before you begin.

Stitch key: The stitch key gives the symbol, the name, the abbreviation if needed, and the instructions for each stitch or group of stitches. When needed, it also gives the instructions for working a particular stitch on the wrong side of the fabric. Be sure to follow these wrong-side instructions when working a wrong-side row.

Slipped stitches: Many of the projects call for slipping stitches along the edge of the knitting to create a tidy selvage stitch. There are almost as many ways to do this as there are knitters. As long as you are getting elongated stitches along the edge of the fabric, you're doing it right!

One approach that works for most people is to always slip the first stitch as if to purl with your yarn held to the wrong side of the fabric. If you find that's not working for the way you knit, you can also try holding the yarn to the back of the work and slipping as if to knit on right-side rows and holding the yarn to the front of the work and slipping as if to purl on wrong-side rows.

Stitch markers: Most patterns suggest using a stitch marker to indicate the beginning of the round. This is optional, but it can make it easier to see exactly what you are doing. If you find them helpful, you may also wish to use stitch markers to separate pattern repeats or to divide the front and back of a sock.

Toes: Several of the socks have a bit of ribbing or other patterning on the toes. If you find that bothers your toes, you can always substitute stockinette or reversed stockinette instead.

It is easy to adjust the shape of the toes to fit your feet. Most of the socks here have you decrease every other row until half your decreases are done and then decrease every round. If you've got pointy toes, you may want to decrease every other round until closer to three quarters of your decreases are done. If you've got flatter toes, you may want to decrease every other round until only one quarter of your decreases are done.

Wrong side: The wrong side of your knitting is the inside or the private side. It is abbreviated WS throughout the text.

Yarn requirements: Each pattern lists the approximate yardage used for the project shown. This is a good guideline, but estimating yardage requirements is a bit of a black art. If you decide to make the leg of your sock 10 inches tall or to make your fingerless gloves elbow length, you're going to need more yarn. When in doubt, buy extra! It's much easier to return an unneeded skein (or add it to the stash) than to run out on the last row.

STITCH KEY

Single Stitches

Symbol	Right Side	Wrong Side	Abbreviation
│	Knit.	Purl.	k
⅃	Knit through the back loop.		ktbl
⊓⊓	Knit, wrapping the yarn around the needle twice.		
⋒	Knit below: Knit into the stitch below.		
—	Purl.	Knit.	p
⊣	Purl through the back loop.	Knit through the back loop.	ptbl
⋁	Purl together: Purl the next stitch together with the long strand at its base.		
○	Yarn over.	Yarn over.	yo
→	Slip: Slip as if to purl with yarn to inside or wrong side of object.	Slip as if to purl with yarn to inside or wrong side of object.	sl
⋂	Slip forward: Slip as if to purl with yarn in front.		
▓	No stitch: Indicates a square on the chart that does not correspond to a stitch. Do nothing. Proceed to the next chart symbol.		

Single Decreases

Symbol	Right Side	Wrong Side	Abbreviation
	Right leaning knit decrease: Knit 2 together.	Purl 2 together.	k2tog
	Right leaning purl decrease: Purl 2 together.		p2tog
	Right leaning twisted knit decrease: Slip 1 knitwise. Slip another 1 knitwise. Return the slipped stitches to the left needle. Knit 2 together.		
	Left leaning knit decrease: Slip 1 knitwise. Slip another 1 knitwise. Return slipped stitches to the left needle. Insert the right needle from the right to the left into the back loops of both stitches. Knit both together.	Slip 1 knitwise. Slip another 1 knitwise. Return slipped stitches to the left needle. Purl 2 together through the back loops.	ssk
	Left leaning purl decrease: Slip 1 knitwise. Slip another 1 knitwise. Return slipped stitches to the left needle. Purl 2 together through the back loops.		ssp
	Left leaning twisted knit decrease: Insert the right needle from the right to the left into the back loops of 2 stitches. Knit both together.		

Double Decreases

Symbol	Right Side
人	Right leaning double knit decrease: Slip 1 knitwise. Slip another 1 knitwise. Return slipped stitches to the left needle. Insert the right needle from the right to the left into the back loops of both stitches. Knit both together. Put the resulting stitch back on the left needle. Pass the second stitch on the left needle over the first. Slip the first stitch back to the right needle.
入	Left leaning double knit decrease: Slip 1 knitwise. Knit 2 together. Pass slipped stitch over.
木	Centered double knit decrease: Slip 2 together at the same time as if to knit 2 together. Knit 1. Pass the slipped stitches over.
人	Centered twisted double knit decrease: Slip 1 as if to purl. Remount next stitch so it is rotated 180 degrees (one half turn) clockwise. Slip the first stitch back to the left needle. Slip 2 together at the same time as if to knit 2 together. Knit 1. Pass the slipped stitches over.

Single Increases

Symbol	Right Side	Wrong Side	Abbreviation
Y	Make 1 left knitwise: With the left needle, lift the strand of yarn between the last stitch you worked and the stitch you would normally work next from the front to the back. Knit into the back of the loop created by the strand of yarn you just picked up.		mll
Y	Make 1 left purlwise: With the left needle, lift the strand of yarn between the last stitch you worked and the stitch you would normally work next from the front to the back. Purl into the back of the loop created by the strand of yarn you just picked up.		
Y	Make 1 right knitwise: With the left needle, lift the strand of yarn between the last stitch you worked and the stitch you would normally work next from the back to the front. Knit into the loop created by the strand of yarn you just picked up.		mlr
Y	Make 1 right purlwise: With the left needle, lift the strand of yarn between the last stitch you worked and the stitch you would normally work next from the back to the front. Purl into the loop created by the strand of yarn you just picked up.		

Double Increases

Symbol	Right Side
▽	Make 1 right purlwise. Purl 1. Make 1 left purlwise.

Multiple Stitches

Symbol	Right Side
	Cluster right: Slip 1, knit 3, pass slipped stitch over 3 knit stitches.
	Cluster left: Knit 3, put 3 stitches back on the left needle. Pass the 4th stitch on the left needle over the 3 stitches you just moved. Slip 3 stitches back to the right needle.
	1x4 Cable, right: Slip 4 to cable needle, hold in back, knit 1, knit 4 from cable needle.
	1x3 Cable, right: Slip 3 to cable needle, hold in back, knit 1, knit 3 from cable needle.
	1x2 Cable, right: Slip 2 to cable needle, hold in back, knit 1, knit 2 from cable needle.
	1x1 Cable, right: Slip 1 to cable needle, hold in back, knit 1, knit 1 from cable needle.
	1x4 Cable, left: Slip 1 to cable needle, hold in front, knit 4, knit 1 from cable needle.
	1x3 Cable, left: Slip 1 to cable needle, hold in front, knit 3, knit 1 from cable needle.
	1x2 Cable, left: Slip 1 to cable needle, hold in front, knit 2, knit 1 from cable needle.
	1x1 Cable, left: Slip 1 to cable needle, hold in front, knit 1, knit 1 from cable needle.
	1x1 Cable, variable: On the left sock, work a 1x1 cable right. On the right sock, work a 1x1 cable left.

CROCUS VERNUS

Crocuses are one of my favorite flowers. The sight of their colorful buds pushing through the snow is a welcome reminder that warmer weather and longer days are on the way. I was thrilled to find such a lovely image of a crocus to work with. The lace on the sock echoes the clean, simple lines of the crocus flower. They are, perhaps, a bit too lacy for the chilliest of early spring days. But if you're anything like me, the weather will have warmed just enough by the time you're finished knitting them. The mitts offer something closer to instant gratification. Their simple shape and easy lace (inspired by the dramatic shape of the leaves) are quick to work while their length makes them just perfect for keeping your hands comfortable on cool days.

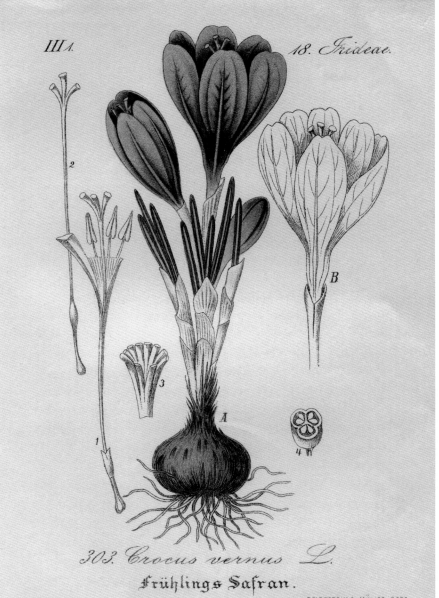

III A.   18. Irideae.

303. Crocus vernus L.
Frühlings Safran.

REIBESTEIN & MÜLLER, GERA.

CROCUS VERNUS SOCK

Shown in: Sock Plus 8 by Handwerks in the color Misty Morning.
Made in size small with about 300 yards of yarn.
Gauge and sizing: 8 stitches in 1 inch in stockinette. Fits a leg or foot
of about 8 [9] inches.

Cast on: Cast on 60 [68] stitches. Place marker and join for working in the round.

Cuff and leg: Throughout the sock, work only the unshaded columns for the smaller size and work both the shaded and unshaded columns for the larger size. Work the Cuff Chart once. Work the Main Chart until sock reaches desired height. Stop after completing row 10 of the Main Chart.

Heel flap: The heel flap is worked over stitches 32-60 [36-68]. It uses a total of 29 [33] stitches.

Row 1 is a wrong-side row (worked with the inside of the sock facing you, following the wrong-side notations in the stitch key, and reading the chart from left to right). Row 2 is a right-side row (worked with the outside of the sock facing you, following the right-side notations in the stitch key, and reading the chart from right to left). Work the appropriate Heel Chart 14 [16] times or until heel flap reaches desired length.

Heel turn: Odd rows are wrong-side rows (worked with the inside of the sock facing you). Even rows are right-side rows (worked with the outside of the sock facing you). Turn at the end of each row.

Row 1 (WS): Sl1, p15 [17], p2tog, p1.
Row 2 (RS): Sl1, k4, ssk, k1.
Row 3 (WS): Sl1, p5, p2tog, p1.
Row 4 (RS): Sl1, k6, ssk, k1.

Row 5 (WS): Sl1, p7, p2tog, p1.
Row 6 (RS): Sl1, k8, ssk, k1.
Row 7 (WS): Sl1, p9, p2tog, p1.
Row 8 (RS): Sl1, k10, ssk, k1.
Row 9 (WS): Sl1, p11, p2tog, p1.
Row 10 (RS): Sl1, k12, ssk, k1.
Row 11 (WS): Sl1, p13, p2tog, p1.
Row 12 (RS): Sl1, k14, ssk, k1.

Large, as above plus:
Row 13 (WS): Sl1, p15, p2tog, p1.
Row 14 (RS): Sl1, k16, ssk, k1.

17 [19] stitches remain.

Gusset and foot:
Setup round: Pick up and knit 1 stitch in each of the slipped stitches along the side of the heel flap, place first marker. Work across the top of the foot following the first row of the Main Chart for the first 30 [34] stitches, p the 31st [35th] stitch, place second marker. Pick up and knit 1 stitch in each of the slipped stitches along the other side of the heel flap, k8 [9]. The round now begins in the middle of the bottom of the foot.

Decrease round: K until 3 stitches remain before first marker, k2tog, k1. Work across the top of the foot following the next row of the Main Chart for the first 30 [34] stitches, p the 31st [35th] stitch. K1, ssk, k to end of round. 2 stitches decreased.

Non-decrease round: K to first marker. Work across the top of the foot following the next row of the Main Chart for the first 30 [34] stitches, p the 31st [35th] stitch. K to end of round.

Alternate decrease and non-decrease rounds until 62 [70] stitches remain. Repeat the non-decrease round until sock measures 3.5 [4] inches shorter than desired length. Stop after completing row 10 of the Main Chart. Work the Toe Chart once. Repeat row 11 of the Toe Chart as needed until the sock is 2 [2.25] inches shorter than desired length.

Toe:
Decrease round: K until 3 stitches remain before first marker, k2tog, k1. P1, ssk, follow ribbing as established by row 11 of the Toe Chart until

3 stitches remain before second marker, k2tog, p1. K1, ssk, k to end of round. 4 stitches decreased.

Non-decrease round: K to first marker. Following rib as established by row 11 of the Toe Chart to second marker. K to end of round.

Work these 2 rounds 5 [7] times, 42 stitches remain. Work the decrease round 6 more times, 18 stitches remain. K to marker. Remove markers. Graft toes. Weave in ends.

Stitch Key

	RS: Knit WS: Purl
—	RS: Purl WS: Knit
O	Yarn over
→	RS: Slip WS: Slip
/	Right leaning knit decrease
\	Left leaning knit decrease
⋏	Make 1 right knitwise
⋎	Make 1 left knitwise

Chart notes: The shaded stitches are used to adjust sizing. Throughout the sock, work only the unshaded columns for the smaller size and work both the shaded and unshaded columns for the larger size.

Cuff Chart

Main Chart

Heel Chart

Toe Chart

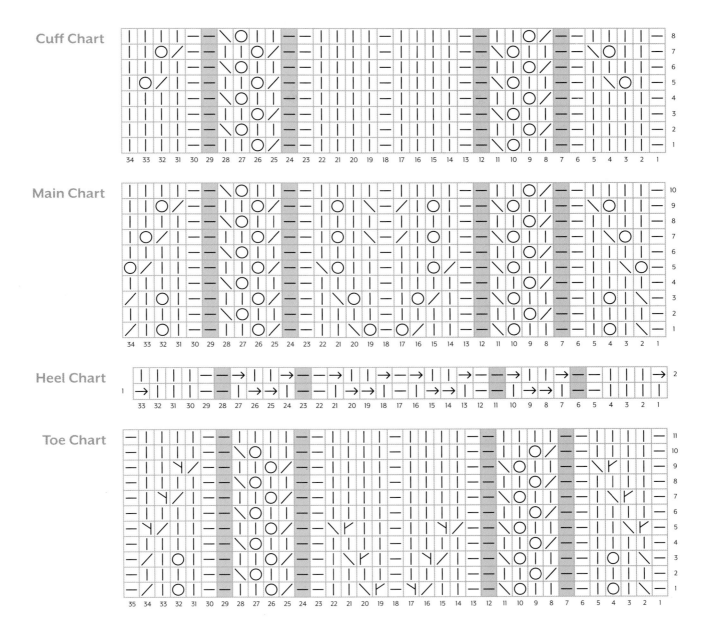

CROCUS VERNUS MITT

Shown in: So-Soft DK by Handwerks in the color Lemongrass. Made in size medium with about 130 yards of yarn.
Gauge and sizing: 6 stitches in 1 inch in stockinette. Fits an arm of about 6.5 [8.5, 10.5] Inches. Measure at the widest part of the arm that you want the mitt to cover.

Cast on: Cast on 36 [48, 60] stitches. Place marker and join for working in the round.

Wrist: Work the Main Chart until wrist reaches desired length (measured to the base of the palm). On the first repeat of the Main Chart, work the gray shaded squares as purl stitches. On subsequent repeats of the Main Chart, work them as shown. Stop after completing row 17 of the Main Chart. On the very last stitch of row 17, work a purl into the front and back (this isn't indicated on the chart). This creates 1 extra stitch. Slip that 1 extra stitch to the next needle. This stitch is shown in column 1 of the Thumb Chart.

Thumb hole: You will now begin working flat instead of in the round. Row 1 and all other odd rows are wrong-side rows (worked with the inside of the mitt facing you, following the wrong-side notations in the stitch key, and reading the chart from left to right). Row 2 and all other even rows are right-side rows (worked with the outside of the mitt facing you, following the right-side notations in the stitch key, and reading the chart from right to left). Work the Thumb Chart once. The gray shaded stitches are worked 2 [3, 4] times. The last stitch of row 22 of the Thumb Chart is a decrease that joins the mitt for working in the round again and decreases away the extra stitch that you added when you began working back and forth.

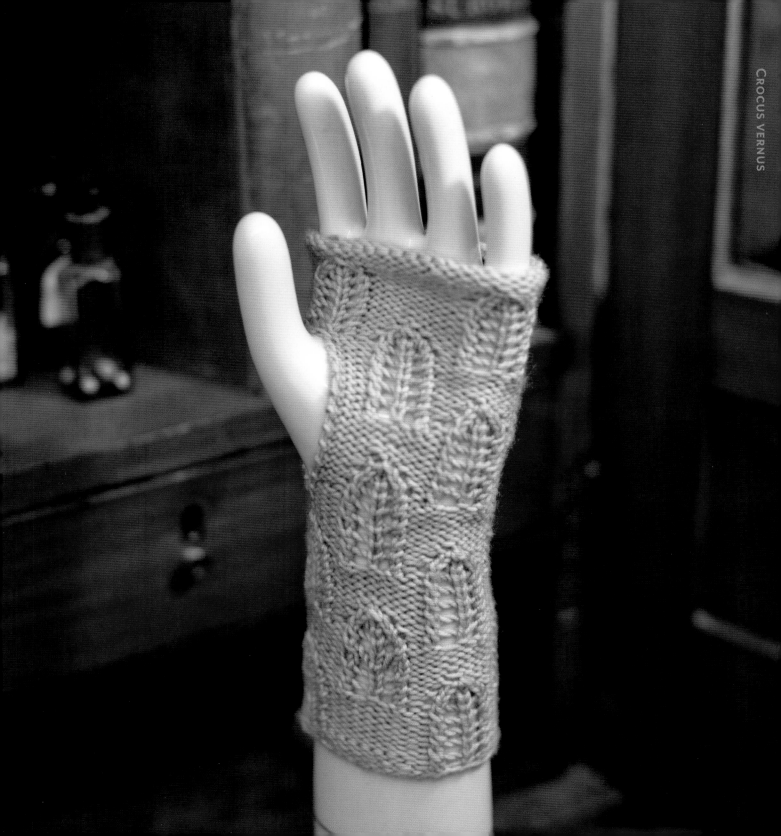

Hand: You will now begin working in the round again. Work 1 repeat of the Hand Chart.

Finishing: Bind off loosely. Weave in ends. Block if desired.

Stitch Key

| | RS: Knit
WS: Purl |
| --- | --- |

RS: Knit
WS: Purl

— RS: Purl
WS: Knit

O Yarn over

→ RS: Slip
WS: Slip

／ Right leaning knit decrease

＼ Left leaning knit decrease

＼ Left leaning purl decrease

∧ Centered double knit decrease

Ｌ Make 1 right purlwise

Ｊ Make 1 left purlwise

Main Chart

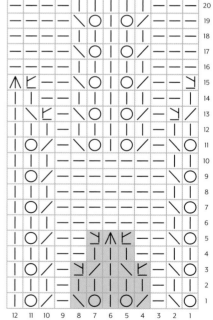

Thumb Chart

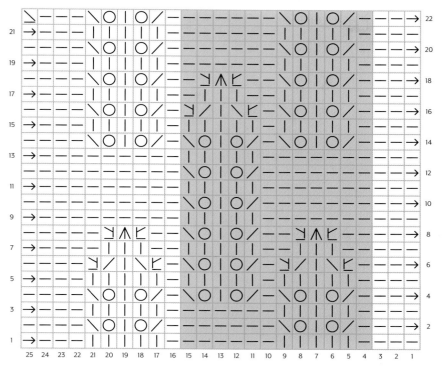

Hand Chart

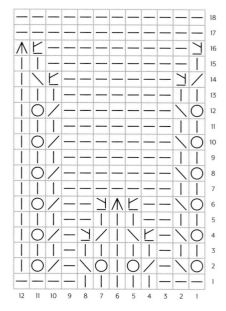

Chart notes: The shaded stitches in the Main Chart are worked differently on the first repeat of the Main Chart. On the first repeat of the Main Chart, work the gray shaded squares as purl stitches. On subsequent repeats of the Main Chart, work them as shown.

The shaded stitches in the Thumb Chart are used to adjust sizing. The gray shaded stitches are worked 2 [3, 4] times.

CHRYSANTHEMUM FRUTESCENS

I sometimes think daisies are a bit underappreciated. They seem so sweet and cheerful that it's easy to forget just how lovely they are. For these socks, I wanted to make something a bit more sophisticated than what you might expect from the common daisy. The curved picot cuff, intricate leg patterning (inspired by the shape of the petals), and careful heel and toe details all combine to produce an unabashedly ornate result. I took the opposite approach for the hat. I kept the shape as simple as possible and used just one beautifully textured stitch (drawn from the pattern on the flower buds) to do all the work. The result is both striking and versatile, producing a hat that works as well for men as for women.

MARGUERITE OR PARIS DAISY
(A) *White:* CHRYSANTHEMUM FRUTESCENS
(B) *Yellow:* CHRYSANTHEMUM FRUTESCENS—*var. chrysaster*
²/₃ Nat. size
PL. 147

CHRYSANTHEMUM FRUTESCENS SOCK

Shown in: Bugga! by Cephalopod Yarns in the color Oleander Nymph. Made in size small with about 320 yards of yarn.
Gauge and sizing: 8 stitches in 1 inch in stockinette. Fits a foot or leg of about 8.5 [9.5] inches.

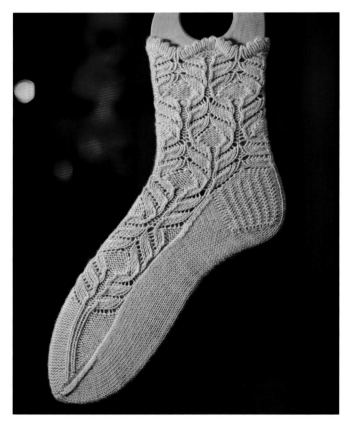

Cast on: Using smaller needles and a provisional cast on, cast on 64 [72] stitches. Place marker and join for working in the round.

Cuff and leg: Using needles 1 size smaller than needed to get gauge, work 6 rounds of k. Work 1 round of yo, k2tog. Switch to larger needles. Work 6 rounds of k. Work the cast on stitches together with the live stitches by knitting each live stitch together with 1 cast on stitch. Work 1 round of k. If you would like a shorter sock, work the appropriate Main Chart once. Stop after completing row 38 [44] of the appropriate Main Chart. If you would like a taller sock, work the appropriate Main Chart one and a half times. Stop after completing row 19 [22] of the appropriate Main Chart.

Heel flap: The heel flap is worked over stitches 34-64 [38-72]. It uses a total of 31 [35] stitches.

Row 1 is a wrong-side row (worked with the inside of the sock facing you, following the wrong-side notations in the stitch key, and reading the chart from left to right). Row 2 is a right-side row (worked with the outside of the sock facing you, following the right-side notations in the stitch key, and reading the chart from right to left). Work the appropriate Heel Chart 15 [17] times or until flap reaches desired height. Be sure you are following the appropriate Short Heel Chart if you are making the shorter sock and the appropriate Tall Heel Chart if you are making the taller sock.

Heel turn: Odd rows are wrong-side rows (worked with the inside of the sock facing you). Even rows are right-side rows (worked with the outside of the sock facing you). Turn at the end of each row.

Row 1 (WS): Sl1, p17 [19], p2tog, p1.
Row 2 (RS): Sl1, k6, ssk, k1.
Row 3 (WS): Sl1, p7, p2tog, p1.
Row 4 (RS): Sl1, k8, ssk, k1.
Row 5 (WS): Sl1, p9, p2tog, p1.
Row 6 (RS): Sl1, k10, ssk, k1.
Row 7 (WS): Sl1, p11, p2tog, p1.
Row 8 (RS): Sl1, k12, ssk, k1.
Row 9 (WS): Sl1, p13, p2tog, p1.
Row 10 (RS): Sl1, k14, ssk, k1.
Row 11 (RS): Sl1, p15, p2tog, p1.
Row 12 (WS): Sl1, k16, ssk, k1.

Large, as above plus:
Row 13 (WS): Sl1, p17, p2tog, p1.
Row 14 (RS): Sl1, k18, ssk, k1.

19 [21] stitches remain.

Gusset and foot:
Setup round: Pick up and knit 1 stitch in each of the slipped stitches along the side of the heel flap, place first marker. Work across the top of the foot following the next row of the appropriate Main Chart (row 1 for the short sock, row 20 [23] for the tall sock) for the first 32 [36] stitches, p the 33rd [37th] stitch, place second marker. Pick up and knit 1 stitch in each of the slipped stitches along the other side of the heel flap, k9 [10]. The round now begins in the middle of the bottom of the foot.

Decrease round: K until 3 stitches remain before first marker, k2tog, k1. Work across the top of the foot following the next row of the appropriate Main Chart for the first 32 [36] stitches, p the 33rd [37th] stitch. K1, ssk, k to end of round. 2 stitches decreased.

Non-decrease round: K to first marker. Work across the top of the foot following the next row of the appropriate Main Chart for the first 32 [36] stitches, p the 33rd [37th] stitch. K to end of round.

Alternate decrease and non-decrease rounds until 66 [74] stitches remain. Repeat the non-decrease round until sock measures 2 [2.5] inches shorter than desired length. End after completing row 38 [44] of the appropriate Main Chart. Repeat row 38 [44] of the appropriate Main Chart as needed to adjust length.

Toe:
Decrease round: K until 3 stitches remain before first marker, k2tog, k1. P1, ssp, follow ribbing as established by row 38 [44] of the appropriate Main Chart until 3 stitches remain before second marker, p2tog, p1. K1, ssk, k to end of round. 4 stitches decreased.

Non-decrease round: K to first marker. Following rib as established by row 38 [44] of the appropriate Main Chart to second marker. K to end of round.

Work these 2 rounds 6 [8] times, 42 stitches remain. Work the decrease round 6 more times, 18 stitches remain. K to marker. Remove markers. Graft toes. Weave in ends.

Stitch Key

	RS: Knit WS: Purl
—	RS: Purl WS: Knit
O	Yarn over
→	RS: Slip WS: Slip
/	Right leaning knit decrease
\	Left leaning knit decrease

Chart notes: The sizes use different charts. Be sure to follow the appropriate chart.

Small Main Chart

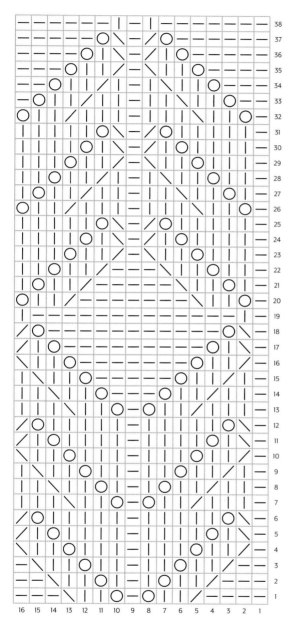

Large Main Chart

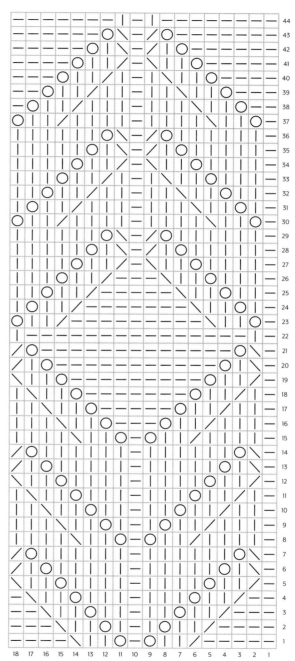

Small Short Heel Chart

31 30 29 28 27 26 25 24 23 22 21 20 19 18 17 16 15 14 13 12 11 10 9 8 7 6 5 4 3 2 1

Small Tall Heel Chart

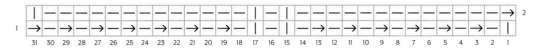

31 30 29 28 27 26 25 24 23 22 21 20 19 18 17 16 15 14 13 12 11 10 9 8 7 6 5 4 3 2 1

Large Short Heel Chart

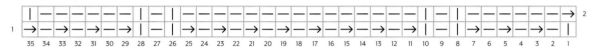

35 34 33 32 31 30 29 28 27 26 25 24 23 22 21 20 19 18 17 16 15 14 13 12 11 10 9 8 7 6 5 4 3 2 1

Large Tall Heel Chart

35 34 33 32 31 30 29 28 27 26 25 24 23 22 21 20 19 18 17 16 15 14 13 12 11 10 9 8 7 6 5 4 3 2 1

Chart notes: The Heel Charts are different depending on the size of sock and the height of leg. Be sure to follow the appropriate chart.

CHRYSANTHEMUM FRUTESCENS HAT

Shown in: Traveller by Verdant Gryphon in the color Ireland. Made in size medium with about 175 yards of yarn.
Gauge and sizing: 20 stitches in 5 inches in Main Chart pattern. Fits a head of 20 [22, 24] inches.
Notes: The pattern is difficult to see until you have worked 2 full repeats of the Main Chart. Don't worry if you don't see it right away.

Cast on: Using needles 2 sizes larger than needed to get gauge, cast on 76 [84, 92] stitches. Place marker and join for working in the round.

Body: The shaded stitches are used to adjust sizing. On all charts, work only the unshaded stitches for the smaller size. Work the unshaded stitches and the light gray stitches for the medium size. Work all stitches for the larger size.

Work the Cuff Chart once. Switch to smaller needles. Work the Main Chart until hat reaches desired height before the decreases. Stop after completing row 4 of the Main Chart

Decreases: Work the Decrease Chart once.

Finishing: Draw the yarn through remaining stitches. Weave in ends. Block if desired.

Stitch Key

| | Knit

⅄ Knit through the back loop

∩ Knit below

— Purl

⋁ Purl together

→ Slip

⋋ Left leaning twisted knit decrease

Chart notes: The shaded stitches are used to adjust sizing. On all charts, work only the unshaded stitches for the smaller size. Work the unshaded stitches and the light gray stitches for the medium size. Work all stitches for the larger size.

Cuff Chart

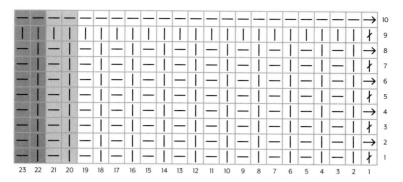

Main Chart

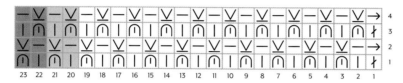

Decrease Chart

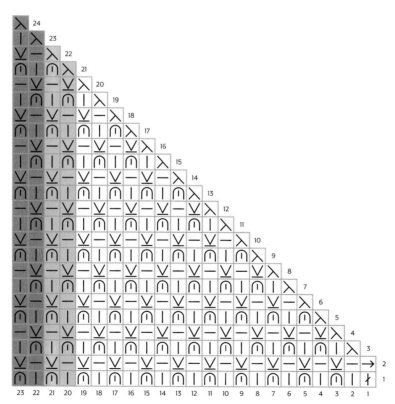

RUBUS SUBERECTUS

This plant is the wild cousin to both blackberries and raspberries, and I have it on good authority that the fruit tastes just as good as you might expect. I debated including any food plants in this collection. There are so many of them that they could easily demand their own project if not carefully watched. But this plant is not cultivated commercially, and it seemed too charming to leave out. The socks echo the simple, almost sparse petals of the flower. The design is easy to work despite its impressive appearance. The shawl is inspired by the beautiful round berries. The intricate bottom border is a bit of a challenge (it's true lace, worked on both right and wrong sides), but it soon gives way to a simple stockinette body and a picot hem. The combination is charming.

2572.

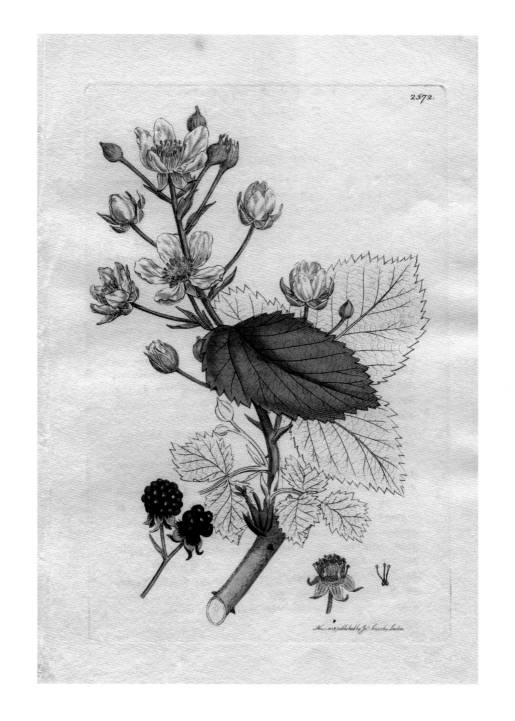

Nov. 1. 1813 published by Ja.s Sowerby London

RUBUS SUBERECTUS SOCK

Shown in: Socks that Rock Mediumweight by Blue Moon Fiber Arts in the color Ghillie Dhu. Made in size small with about 325 yards of yarn.
Gauge and sizing: 8 stitches in 1 inch in stockinette. Fits a foot or leg of about 7.5 [10] inches.
Notes: The larger size is a bit large at the listed gauge. If you want a smaller sock, you may use a finer yarn at a tighter gauge.

Cast on: Cast on 60 [80] stitches. Place marker and join for working in the round.

Cuff and leg: Work the Cuff Chart once. Work it as follows: Work columns 1-5 3 [4] times then work columns 6-10 3 [4] times. Work columns 1-5 3 [4] times then work columns 6-10 3 [4] times. Work the Main Chart until sock reaches desired height. Work it as follows: Work columns 1-5 3 [4] times then work columns 6-10 3 [4] times. Work columns 1-5 3 [4] times then work columns 6-10 3 [4] times. Stop after completing row 6 of the Main Chart.

Heel flap: The heel flap is worked over stitches 32-60 [42-80]. It uses a total of 29 [39] stitches.

Row 1 is a wrong-side row (worked with the inside of the sock facing you). Row 2 is a right-side row (worked with the outside of the sock facing you). Work these two rows 13 [18] times or until flap reaches desired length.

Row 1 (WS): Sl1, p3, (k1, p4) 5 [7] times.
Row 2 (RS): Sl1, k3, (p1, k4) 5 [7] times.

Heel turn: Odd rows are wrong-side rows (worked with the inside of the sock facing you). Even rows are right-side rows (worked with the outside of the sock facing you). Turn at the end of each row.

Row 1 (WS): Sl1, p15 [21], p2tog, p1.
Row 2 (RS): Sl1, k4 [6], ssk, k1.
Row 3 (WS): Sl1, p5 [7], p2tog, p1.
Row 4 (RS): Sl1, k6 [8], ssk, k1.
Row 5 (WS): Sl1, p7 [9], p2tog, p1.
Row 6 (RS): Sl1, k8 [10], ssk, k1.
Row 7 (WS): Sl1, p9 [11], p2tog, p1.
Row 8 (RS): Sl1, k10 [12], ssk, k1.
Row 9 (WS): Sl1, p11 [13], p2tog, p1.
Row 10 (RS): Sl1, k12 [14], ssk, k1.
Row 11 (WS): Sl1, p13 [15], p2tog, p1.
Row 12 (RS): Sl1, k14 [16], ssk, k1.

Large, as above plus:
Row 13 (WS): Sl1, p—[17], p2tog, p1.
Row 14 (RS): Sl1, k—[18], ssk, k1.
Row 15 (WS): Sl1, p—[19], p2tog, p1.
Row 16 (RS): Sl1, k—[20], ssk, k1.

17 [23] stitches remain.

Gusset and foot:
Setup round: Pick up and knit 1 stitch in each of the slipped stitches along the side of the heel flap, place first marker. Work across the top of the foot following the first row of the Main Chart for the first 30 [40] stitches. Work the Main Chart as follows: Work columns 1-5 3 [4] times then work columns 6-10 3 [4] times. P the 31st [41st] stitch, place second marker. Pick up and knit 1 stitch in each of the slipped stitches along the other side of the heel flap, k9 [12]. The round now begins in the middle of the bottom of the foot.

Decrease round: K until 3 stitches remain before first marker, k2tog, k1. Work across the top of the foot following the next row of the Main Chart as described above for the first 30 [40] stitches, p the 31st [41st] stitch. K1, ssk, k to end of round. 2 stitches decreased.

Non-decrease round: K to first marker. Work across the top of the foot following the next row of the Main Chart as described above for the first 30 [40] stitches, p the 31st [41st] stitch. K to end of round.

Alternate decrease and non-decrease rounds until 62 [82] stitches remain. Repeat the non-decrease round until sock measures 2 [2.75]

inches shorter than desired length. Stop after completing row 6 of the Main Chart. Repeat row 1 of the Main Chart as needed to adjust length.

Toe:
Decrease round: K until 3 stitches remain before first marker, k2tog, k1. P1, ssk, follow ribbing as established by row 1 of the Main Chart until 3 stitches remain before second marker, k2tog, p1. K1, ssk, k to end of round. 4 stitches decreased.

Non-decrease round: K to first marker. Follow ribbing as established by row 1 of the Main Chart to the second marker. K to end of round.

Work these 2 rounds 5 [10] times, 42 stitches remain. Work the decrease round 6 more times, 18 stitches remain. K to marker. Remove markers. Graft toes. Weave in ends.

Stitch Key

| | Knit

Ⓜ Knit, wrapping yarn around needle twice

— Purl

◯ Yarn over

→ Slip, dropping the extra loop

Cluster right

Cluster left

Chart notes: The charts are read in a slightly unusual way. Pay close attention to the instructions.

Main Chart

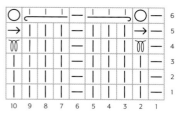

Cuff Chart

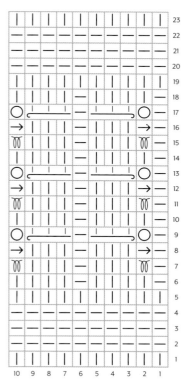

RUBUS SUBERECTUS SHAWL

Shown in: Woobu by Blue Moon Fiber Arts in the color Jasper. Made in size medium with about 425 yards of yarn.
Gauge and sizing: 5 stitches in 1 inch in stockinette. After blocking, the shawl is about 40 [46, 52] inches across at the top edge.

Cast on: Cast on 194 [218, 242] stitches.

Edging: For all charts, work column 1. Work columns 2-13 16 [18, 20] times. Work column 14 once. Columns 1 and 14 are shaded to remind you to only work them once.

Row 1 and all other odd rows are wrong-side rows (worked with the inside of the shawl facing you, following the wrong-side notations in the stitch key, and reading the chart from left to right). Row 2 and all other even rows are right-side rows (worked with the outside of the shawl facing you, following the right-side notations in the stitch key, and reading the chart from right to left).

Lower edging: Work the Main Chart 5 times.

Transition: Work the Transition Chart once.

Body: Odd rows are wrong-side rows (worked with the inside of the shawl facing you). Even rows are right-side rows (worked with the outside of the shawl facing you). Turn at the end of each row.

Row 1 (WS): sl1, p100 [112, 124].
Row 2 (RS): sl1, k7.
Row 3 (WS): sl1, p6, ssp, p3.
Row 4 (RS): sl1, k9, k2tog, k3.
Row 5 (WS): sl1, p12, ssp, p3.
Row 6 (RS): sl1, k15, k2tog, k3.

Continue to work rows 5 and 6, adding 3 to the central stretch of stockinette each row (so p18 on row 7, k21 on row 8, p24 on row 9, k27 on row 10 etc). Work these 2 rows until all stitches are used. On the last repeat, there may not be 3 stitches left to work at the very end, just work any stitches that are there.

Upper edging: Work 5 rows of stockinette, slipping the first stitch of each row. Work 1 row of k2tog, yo. Work 4 rows of stockinette, slipping the first stitch of each row. Work 1 final row of stockinette, spacing 6 decreases evenly across the row.

Finishing: Bind off loosely, weave in ends. Fold fabric over on the k2tog, yo row and stitch down the edge. Block if desired.

Stitch Key

| | RS: Knit / WS: Purl

⅄ Knit through the back loop

O | RS: Yarn over / WS: Yarn over

→ | RS: Slip / WS: Slip

╱ | RS: Right leaning knit decrease / WS: Left leaning purl decrease

╲ | RS: Left leaning knit decrease / WS: Right leaning purl decrease

⋀ Centred double knit decrease

Chart notes: The shaded stitches are the edge stitches, the unshaded stitches are repeated.

Main Chart

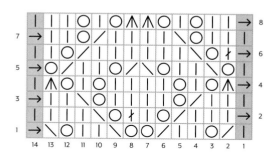

Transition Chart

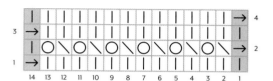

PINUS SILVESTRIS

Flowers are showy; they get all the attention. But plants that don't make what we think of as flowers can be just as lovely as their flashier counterparts. I wanted to be sure to include at least a few of them in this collection, and the Scots pine is a perfect example. The socks are simple stockinette with a decorated panel that runs down the front and back. The panel is mirrored and twists gently around your foot. The pattern on the panel is drawn from the scales on the mature pine cone. The hat is inspired by the amazing orange color and intricate texture of the young pine cone. The decorated band at the bottom produces a lovely wavy edge while the plain crown ensures a comfortable fit. Be sure to peek at the inside of the hat as some people like that even more.

496.

TALL, PINUS SILVESTRIS L.

Gen. Stab. Lit. Anst.

PINUS SILVESTRIS SOCK

Shown in: Silk Crush by Sweet Georgia in the color Deep Olive. Made in size medium with about 275 yards of yarn.
Gauge and sizing: 8 stitches in 1 inch in stockinette. Fits a foot or leg of about 7.5 [8.5, 9.5] inches.
Notes: These socks are mirrored. The gusset decreases happen in an unusual place. Pay close attention to the instructions.

Cast on: 56 [64, 72] stitches. Place marker and join for working in the round.

Left cuff and leg: stitches 11-27 [15-31, 19-35] and 39-55 [47-63, 55-71] are charted. The other 22 [30, 38] stitches are either ribbed or stockinette.

For the cuff, work in p1, ktbl1 ribbing for 10 [14, 18] stitches. Work the Main Chart. Work in ktbl1, p1 ribbing for 11 [15, 19] stitches. Work the Main Chart. Ktbl1. Work the cuff for 8 rounds.

For the leg, work as for the cuff, except work the non-charted stitches as stockinette. Work in this fashion until sock reaches desired height. Stop after completing row 16 of the Main Chart.

Left heel flap: The heel flap is worked over stitches 29-56 [33-64, 37-72]. It uses a total of 28 [32, 36] stitches. Odd rows are wrong-side rows (worked with the inside of the sock facing you, following the wrong-side notations in the stitch key, and reading the chart from left to right). Even rows are right-side rows (worked with the outside of the sock facing you, following the right-side notations in the stitch key, and reading the chart from right to left). Work the Left Heel Chart once. The gray shaded stitches are worked 9 [13, 17] times. Work

rows 1 and 2 of the Left Heel Chart 4 [6, 8] times or until flap reaches desired length.

Right cuff and leg: stitches 2-18 and 30-46 [34-50, 38-54] are charted. The other 22 [30, 38] stitches are either ribbed or stockinette.

For the cuff, ktbl1. Work the Main Chart. Work in ktbl1, p1 ribbing for 11 [15, 19] stitches. Work the Main Chart. Work in ktbl1, p1 ribbing for 10 [14, 18] stitches. Work the cuff for 8 rounds.

For the leg, work as for the cuff, except work the non-charted stitches as stockinette. Work in this fashion until sock reaches desired height. Stop after completing row 16 of the Main Chart.

Right heel flap: The heel flap is worked over stitches 29-56 [33-64, 37-72]. It uses a total of 28 [32, 36] stitches. Odd rows are wrong-side rows (worked with the inside of the sock facing you, following the wrong-side notations in the stitch key, and reading the chart from left to right). Even rows are right-side rows (worked with the outside of the sock facing you, following the right-side notations in the stitch key, and reading the chart from right to left). Work the Right Heel Chart once. The gray shaded stitches are worked 9 [13, 17] times. Work rows 1 and 2 of the Right Heel Chart 4 [6, 8] times or until flap reaches desired length.

Heel turn: Odd rows are wrong-side rows (worked with the inside of the sock facing you). Even rows are right-side rows (worked with the outside of the sock facing you). Turn at the end of each row.

Row 1 (WS): Sl1, p16 [18, 20], p2tog, p1.
Row 2 (RS): Sl1, k7, ssk, k1.
Row 3 (WS): Sl1, p8, p2tog, p1.
Row 4 (RS): Sl1, k9, ssk, k1.
Row 5 (WS): Sl1, p10, p2tog, p1.
Row 6 (RS): Sl1, k11, ssk, k1.
Row 7 (WS): Sl1, p12, p2tog, p1.
Row 8 (RS): Sl1, k13, ssk, k1.
Row 9 (WS): Sl1, p14, p2tog, p1.
Row 10 (RS): Sl1, k15, ssk, k1.

Medium and large, as above plus:
Row 11 (WS): Sl1, p16, p2tog, p1.
Row 12 (RS): Sl1, k17, ssk, k1.

Large, as above plus:
Row 13 (WS): Sl1, p18, p2tog, p1.
Row 14 (RS): Sl1, k19, ssk, k1.

18 [20, 22] stitches remain.

Gusset and foot: 17 of the stitches on the top of the foot are charted. The other 11 [15, 19] are stockinette. The gusset decreases happen on either side of the 17 charted stitches. Once the gusset decreases are completed, the charted panel moves across the top of the foot. Please be sure to read both the round descriptions and the section called "Instructions" before you begin!

Left setup round: Pick up and k1 stitch in each of the slipped stitches along the heel flap. K10 [14, 19] stitches, place first marker. Work the first row of the Main Chart, k1. Place second marker. Pick up and k1 stitch in each of the slipped stitches along the heel flap, k9 [10, 11]. The round begins in the middle of the bottom of the foot.

Left decrease round: K until 2 stitches remain before first marker, k2tog. Work the next row of the Main Chart, k1, ssk. K to end of round. 2 stitches decreased.

Left regular round: K to first marker. Work the next row of the Main Chart. K to end of round.

Left shifting round: K until 2 stitches remain before first marker, k2tog. Work the next row of the Main Chart, m1l. K to end of round.

Right setup round: Pick up and k1 stitch in each of the slipped stitches along the heel flap, place first marker. K1, work the first row of the Main Chart, place second marker. K10 [14, 19]. Pick up and k1 stitch in each of the slipped stitches along the heel flap, k9 [10, 11]. The round begins in the middle of the bottom of the foot.

Right decrease round: K until 2 stitches remain before first marker, k2tog. K1, work the next row of the Main Chart, ssk. K to end of round. 2 stitches decreased.

Right regular round: K to first marker. Work across the top of the foot following the next row of the Main Chart. K to end of round.

Right shifting round: Move the first marker 1 stitch to the left (the marker is now immediately before the purl stitch that is stitch 1 in the Main Chart). K to first marker, slip marker, m1r. Work the next row of the Main Chart, ssk. K to end of round.

Instructions: Work the appropriate setup round once. Alternate appropriate decrease round and regular round until 56 [64, 72] stitches remain. End after completing a regular round. Alternate appropriate shifting round and regular round until charted panel reaches the far edge of the sock.

On the left sock, this happens when stitch 1 of the Main Chart is the 15th [17th, 19th] stitch of the round. On the right sock, this happens when stitch 17 of the Main Chart is the 42nd [48th, 54th] stitch of the round.

Repeat the appropriate regular round until the sock is 1.5 [1.75, 2] inches shorter than desired length.

Toe: Arrange markers so that that they evenly divide the top and bottom stitches (stitch 1 of the Main Chart is the first stitch of the top of the left sock, stitch 17 of the Main Chart is the last stitch of the top of the right sock).

Decrease round: K until 3 stitches remain before first marker, k2tog, k1. K1, ssk, k until 3 stitches remain before second marker, k2tog, k1. K1, ssk, k to end of round. 4 stitches decreased.

Non-decrease round: K to end of round.

Work these 2 rounds 4 [6, 8] times, 40 stitches remain. Work the decrease round 6 more times, 16 stitches remain. K to marker. Remove markers. Graft toes. Weave in ends.

Stitch Key

	RS: Knit WS: Purl
—	RS: Purl WS: Knit
O	Yarn over
→	RS: Slip WS: Slip
/	Right leaning knit decrease
\	Left leaning knit decrease
∠	Right leaning purl decrease
∧	Centered double knit decrease

Main Chart

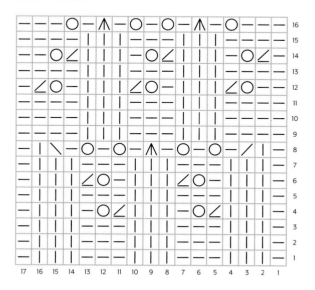

Left Heel Flap Chart

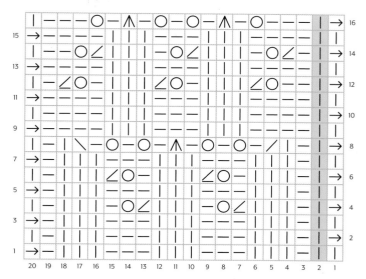

Right Heel Flap Chart

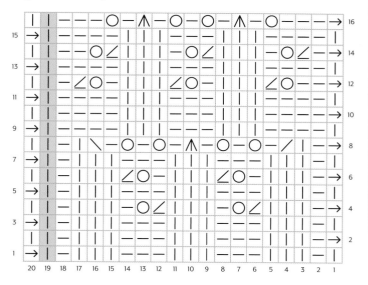

Chart notes: The shaded stitches in the heel flap are used to adjust sizing. Pay close attention to the instructions. The gray shaded stitches are worked 9 [13, 17] times.

PINUS SILVESTRIS HAT

Shown in: Merino Silk Aran by Sweet Georgia in the color Cayenne.
Made in size medium with about 140 yards of yarn.
Gauge and sizing: 20 stitches in 4 inches in stockinette. Fits a head of
20 [22, 24] inches.

Cast on: Cast on 100 [110, 120] stitches. Place marker and join for working in the round.

Body: Work the Main Chart once. 90 [99, 108] stitches remain. Repeat row 24 of the Main Chart until hat reaches desired height before the decreases.

Decreases: Work the Decrease Chart once. Work 1 round of k2tog.

Finishing: Draw the yarn through remaining stitches. Weave in ends. Block if desired.

Stitch Key

| | Knit

— Purl

■ No stitch

/ Right leaning knit decrease

\ Left leaning knit decrease

/\ Centered double knit decrease

∇ Centered double purl increase

Main Chart

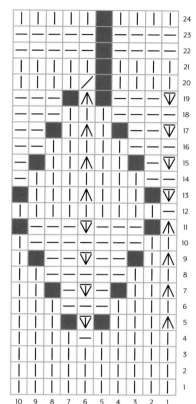

Chart notes: When a centered double decrease is the first stitch on the needle, it requires extra attention. The double decrease turns 3 stitches into 1. When the double decrease happens at the beginning of a needle, the first of those 3 stitches is the last stitch of the previous needle.

For example, the first stitch of round 5 is a centered double decrease. The decrease will use the last stitch of round 4 and the first 2 stitches of round 5. To make the decrease, do not work the last stitch of round 4. Instead, use it as the first of the 3 stitches of the decrease as described in the stitch key. The completed stitch will be the first stitch of round 5.

Decrease Chart

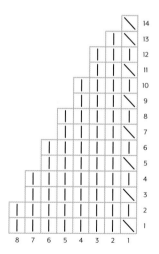

ROSA RUBIGINOSA

I love the contrasts inherent in sweet briar. Delicate, sweet-smelling, pale pink flowers adorn massive shrubs that tower far above your head and are covered in piercing thorns. It's a perfect illustration of the danger of underestimating something just because it seems delicate or demure. The socks echo the subdued form of the petals. Simple and straightforward, they nonetheless give a charming result especially as the patterning falls away leaving plain stockinette on your instep. The mitts are a bit more challenging. An intricate lace panel (inspired by the sharp points of the thorns) runs up the back of the hand. The palm is ribbed to provide a good fit, and the thumb is carefully positioned to ensure the mitt is comfortable.

292.

LUKTTÖRNE, ROSA RUBIGINOSA L.

Gen. Stab. Lit. Anst.

ROSA RUBIGINOSA SOCK

Cast on: Cast on 60 [80] stitches. Place marker and join for working in the round.

Cuff and leg: Work the Cuff Chart once. Work the Main Chart until sock reaches desired height. Stop after completing row 12 of the Main Chart.

Heel flap: The heel flap is worked over stitches 32-60 [42-80]. It uses a total of 29 [39] stitches.

Row 1 is a wrong-side row (worked with the inside of the sock facing you). Row 2 is a right-side row (worked with the outside of the sock facing you). Work these two rows 14 [19] times or until flap reaches desired length.

Row 1 (WS): (Sl1, p1) 14 [19] times, k1.
Row 2 (RS): Sl1, (k1, p1) 14 [19] times.

Heel turn: Odd rows are wrong-side rows (worked with the inside of the sock facing you). Even rows are right-side rows (worked with the outside of the sock facing you). Turn at the end of each row.

Row 1 (WS): Sl1, p15 [21], p2tog, p1.
Row 2 (RS): Sl1, k4 [6], ssk, k1.

Row 3 (WS): Sl1, p5 [7], p2tog, p1.
Row 4 (RS): Sl1, k6 [8], ssk, k1.
Row 5 (WS): Sl1, p7 [9], p2tog, p1.
Row 6 (RS): Sl1, k8 [10], ssk, k1.
Row 7 (WS): Sl1, p9 [11], p2tog, p1.
Row 8 (RS): Sl1, k10 [12], ssk, k1.
Row 9 (WS): Sl1, p11 [13], p2tog, p1.
Row 10 (RS): Sl1, k12 [14], ssk, k1.
Row 11 (WS): Sl1, p13 [15], p2tog, p1.
Row 12 (RS): Sl1, k14 [16], ssk, k1.

Large, as above plus:
Row 13 (WS): Sl1, p—[17], p2tog, p1.
Row 14 (RS): Sl1, k—[18], ssk, k1.
Row 15 (WS): Sl1, p—[19], p2tog, p1.
Row 16 (RS): Sl1, k—[20], ssk, k1.

17 [23] stitches remain.

Gusset and foot:
Setup round: Pick up and knit 1 stitch in each of the slipped stitches along the side of the heel flap, place first marker. Work across the top of the foot following the first row of the Main Chart for the first 30 [40] stitches, k the 31st [41st] stitch, place second marker. Pick up and knit 1 stitch in each of the slipped stitches along the other side of the heel flap, k8 [11]. The round now begins in the middle of the bottom of the foot.

Decrease round: K until 3 stitches remain before first marker, k2tog, k1. Work across the top of the foot following the next row of the Main Chart for the first 30 [40] stitches, k the 31st [41st] st. K1, ssk, k to end of round. 2 stitches decreased

Non-decrease round: K to first marker. Work across the top of the foot following the next row of the Main Chart for the first 30 [40] stitches, k the 31st [41st] stitch. K to end of round.

Alternate decrease and non-decrease rounds until 62 [82] stitches remain. Repeat the non-decrease round until you next finish row 12 of the Main Chart. Work the appropriate Toe Chart once. Repeat the last row of the appropriate Toe Chart until sock measures 2 [2.75] inches shorter than desired length.

Toe:
Decrease round: K until 3 stitches remain before first marker, k2tog, k1. K1, ssk, k until 3 stitches remain before second marker, k2tog, k1. K1, ssk, k to end of round. 4 stitches decreased.

Non-decrease round: K to end of round.

Work these 2 rounds 5 [10] times, 42 stitches remain. Work the decrease round 6 more times, 18 stitches remain. K to marker. Remove markers. Graft toes. Weave in ends.

Stitch Key

| Knit

— Purl

O Yarn over

/ Right leaning knit decrease

\ Left leaning knit decrease

Cuff Chart

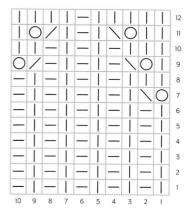

Main Chart

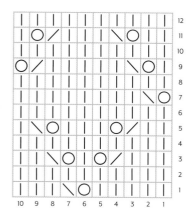

Small Toe Chart

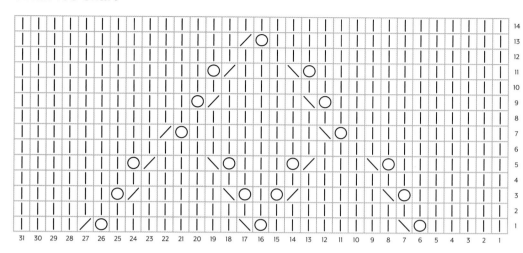

Chart notes: Each size uses a different Toe Chart. Be sure to follow the appropriate chart.

Large Toe Chart

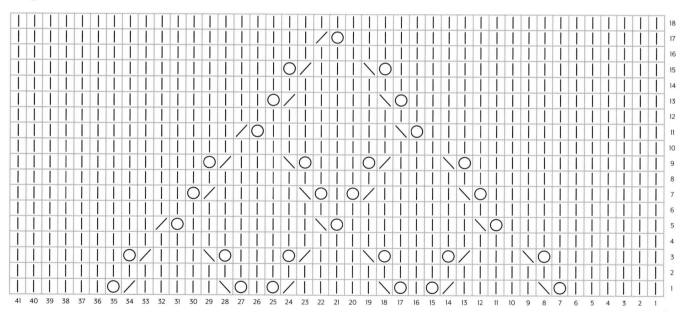

ROSA RUBIGINOSA MITTS

Cast on: Cast on 42 [46, 50, 54] stitches. Place marker and join for working in the round.

Wrist: Work the Main Chart over stitches 1-23. Work the remaining 19 [23, 27, 31] stitches in ktbl1, p1 ribbing. You will begin and end the ribbing with a ktbl. Work the Main Chart until wrist reaches desired length (measured to the base of the palm). Stop after completing row 12 of the Main Chart.

Thumb: To make the thumb gusset, you will gradually create 12 extra stitches.

Right thumb gusset: Work the next row of the Main Chart over stitches 1-23. Ktbl1, p1, ktbl1. Work the next row of the Thumb Chart. Work the next 15 [19, 23, 27] stitches in ktbl1, p1 ribbing. Work through the Main and Thumb Charts in this fashion once. You will have a total of 54 [58, 62, 66] stitches.

Left thumb gusset: Work the next row of the Main Chart over stitches 1-23. Work the next 15 [19, 23, 27] stitches in ktbl1, p1 ribbing. Work the next row of the Thumb Chart. Ktbl1, p1, ktbl1. Work through the Main and Thumb Charts in this fashion once. You will have a total of 54 [58, 62, 66] stitches.

Hand, part 1: Work the Main Chart over stitches 1-23. Work the remaining 31 [35, 39, 43] stitches in ktbl1, p1 ribbing. Work the Main Chart in this fashion once.

Hand, part 2: You will now set aside the stitches for the thumb gusset (the 12 stitches you created and the central p stitch).

Right hand: Locate and set aside stitches 27-39 on a spare needle or length of scrap yarn. Work the next row of the Main Chart over stitches 1-23. Ktbl1, p1, ktbl1, cast on 1 (to make up for the central p stitch you set aside). Work the remaining 15 [19, 23, 27] stitches in ktbl1, p1 ribbing.

Left hand: Locate and set aside stitches 39-51 [43-55, 47-59, 51-63] on a spare needle or length of scrap yarn. Work the next row of the Main Chart over stitches 1-23. Work the next 15 [19, 23, 27] stitches in ktbl1, p1 ribbing. Cast on 1 (to make up for the central p stitch you set aside). Ktbl1, p1, ktbl1.

You will have a total of 42 [46, 50, 54] stitches on your active needles and 13 stitches on a spare needle.

Work the Main Chart over stitches 1-23. Work the remaining 19 [23, 27, 31] stitches in ktbl1, p1 ribbing. Work the Main Chart once. Cast off loosely.

Thumb: Divide the 13 stitches set aside for the thumb across two needles. Pick up 5 [5, 7, 7] stitches to bridge the gap between the first and last of the set aside thumb stitches. You will have 18 [18, 20, 20] thumb stitches. Work in ktbl1, p1 ribbing for 12 rounds.

Finishing: Cast off loosely. Weave in ends. Block if desired.

Stitch Key

| | Knit

ϟ Knit through the back loop

— Purl

O Yarn over

/ Right leaning knit decrease

\ Left leaning knit decrease

Make 1 right knitwise

Make 1 left knitwise

Make 1 right purlwise

Make 1 left purlwise

Main Chart

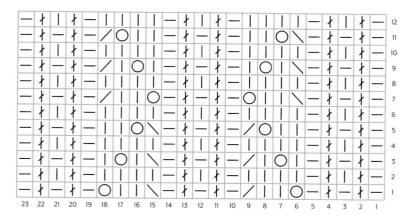

Thumb Chart

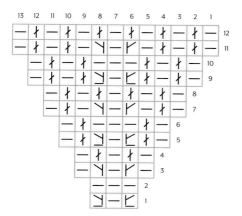

DIANTHUS SUPERBUS

I know it's a bit unrealistic, but I tend to think of plants as being made up of curved lines and rounded forms. Graceful tendrils and fat fruits come to mind more readily than straight lines and sharp edges. So when I saw this image, I was immediately struck by the angular nature of the plants it depicts. I was certain it would inspire interesting projects. There aren't many cables used in this collection, but they seemed like the perfect way to reinterpret the wild exuberance of the frilly petals. They make for an especially striking sock. The cross section of the whole flower provided the starting point for the cowl. I wanted to make something that used only straight lines but still maintained an organic form. I'm thrilled with the result.

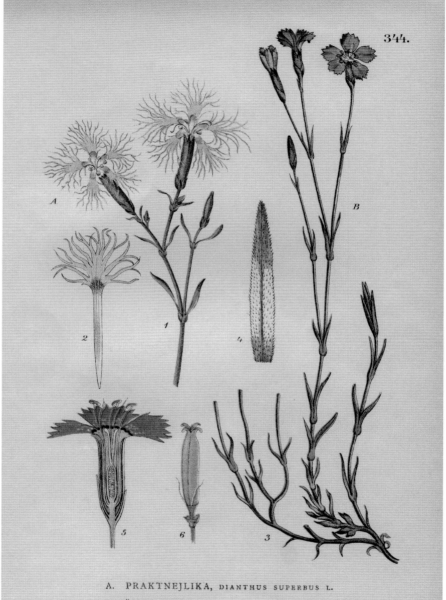

344.

A. PRAKTNEJLIKA, DIANTHUS SUPERBUS L.
B. ÄNGSNEJLIKA, DIANTHUS DELTOIDES L.

Gen. Stab. Lit. Anst.

DIANTHUS SUPERBUS SOCK

Shown in: Nichole by the Schaefer Yarn Company in the color Thistle. Made in size small with about 325 yards of yarn.
Gauge and sizing: 8 stitches in 1 inch in stockinette. Fits a foot or leg of about 7 [9.5] inches.

Cast on: Cast on 60 [80] stitches. Place marker and join for working in the round.

Cuff and leg: Work the Cuff Chart once. For the small left sock, start following the Cuff Chart at column 11 instead of at column 1. Work the Main Chart until sock reaches desired height. For the small left sock, start following the Main Chart at column 11 instead of at column 1. Stop after completing row 12 of the Main Chart.

Heel flap: The heel flap is worked over stitches 32-60 [42-80]. It uses a total of 29 [39] stitches.

Row 1 is a wrong-side row (worked with the inside of the sock facing you). Row 2 is a right-side row (worked with the outside of the sock facing you). Work these 2 rows 14 [19] times or until heel flap reaches desired length.

Row 1 (WS): {(Sl1, p1) 4 times, sl1, k1} 2 [3] times, (sl1, p1) 4 times, p1.
Row 2 (RS): Sl1, k8, (p1, k9) 2 [3] times.

Heel turn: Odd rows are wrong-side rows (worked with the inside of the sock facing you). Even rows are right-side rows (worked with the outside of the sock facing you). Turn at the end of each row.

Row 1 (WS): Sl1, p15 [21], p2tog, p1.
Row 2 (RS): Sl1, k4 [6], ssk, k1.

Row 3 (WS): Sl1, p5 [7], p2tog, p1.
Row 4 (RS): Sl1, k6 [8], ssk, k1.
Row 5 (WS): Sl1, p7 [9], p2tog, p1.
Row 6 (RS): Sl1, k8 [10], ssk, k1.
Row 7 (WS): Sl1, p9 [11], p2tog, p1.
Row 8 (RS): Sl1, k10 [12], ssk, k1.
Row 9 (WS): Sl1, p11 [13], p2tog, p1.
Row 10 (RS): Sl1, k12 [14], ssk, k1.
Row 11 (WS): Sl1, p13 [15], p2tog, p1.
Row 12 (RS): Sl1, k14 [16], ssk, k1.

Large, as above plus:
Row 13 (WS): Sl1, p—[17], p2tog, p1.
Row 14 (RS): Sl1, k—[18], ssk, k1.
Row 15 (WS): Sl1, p—[19], p2tog, p1.
Row 16 (RS): Sl1, k—[20], ssk, k1.

17 [23] stitches remain.

Gusset and foot:
Setup round: Pick up and knit 1 stitch in each of the slipped stitches along the side of the heel flap, place first marker. Work across the top of the foot following the first row of the Main Chart for the first 30 [40] stitches, p the 31st [41st] stitch, place second marker. As on the leg, for the small left sock, start following the Main Chart at column 11 instead of at column 1. Pick up and knit 1 stitch in each of the slipped stitches along the other side of the heel flap, k8 [11]. The round now begins in the middle of the bottom of the foot.

Decrease round: K until 3 stitches remain before first marker, k2tog, k1. Work across the top of the foot following the next row of the Main Chart for the first 30 [40] stitches, p the 31st [41st] stitch. K1, ssk, k to end of round. 2 stitches decreased.

Non-decrease round: K to first marker. Work across the top of the foot following the next row of the Main Chart for the first 30 [40] stitches, p the 31st [41st] stitch. K to end of round.

Alternate decrease and non-decrease rounds until 62 [82] stitches remain. Repeat the non-decrease round until sock measures 3.5 [4.5] inches shorter than desired length. Work the appropriate Toe Chart once. Repeat row 6 [12] of the appropriate Toe Chart until sock measures 2 [2.75] inches shorter than desired length.

Toe:
Decrease round: K until 3 stitches remain before first marker, k2tog, k1. P1, ssk, follow ribbing as established by row 6 [12] of the appropriate Toe Chart until 3 stitches remain before second marker, k2tog, p1. K1, ssk, k to end of round. 4 stitches decreased.

Non-decrease round: K to first marker. Following rib as established by row 6 [12] of the appropriate Toe Chart to second marker. K to end of round.

Work these 2 rounds 5 [10] times, 42 stitches remain. Work the decrease round 6 more times, 18 stitches remain. K to marker. Remove markers. Graft toes. Weave in ends.

Stitch Key

| | Knit

— Purl

| | | | / | 1 by 4 Cable right

| \ | | | | 1 by 4 Cable left

| | | / | 1 by 3 Cable right

| \ | | | 1 by 3 Cable left

| | / | 1 by 2 Cable right

| \ | | 1 by 2 Cable left

| / | 1 by 1 Cable right

| \ | 1 by 1 Cable left

Cuff Chart

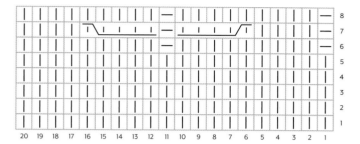

Main Chart

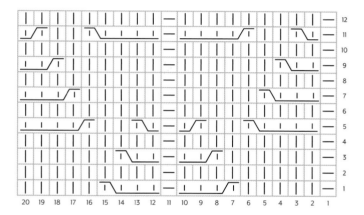

Chart notes: In the small size, the left and right socks are slightly different. The small left sock starts following the Cuff and Main Charts at an unusual point (column 11 instead of column 1).

Small Left Toe Chart

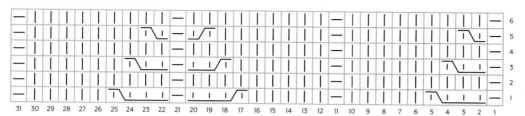

Small Right Toe Chart

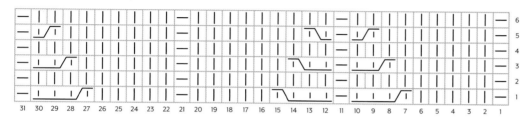

Large Toe Chart

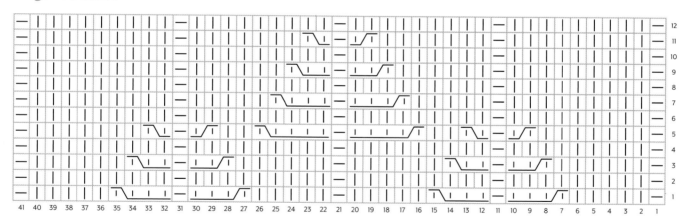

Chart notes: Each size uses a different Toe Chart. Be sure to follow the appropriate chart.

DIANTHUS SUPERBUS COWL

Shown in: Chris by the Schaefer Yarn Company in the color Pomegranate. Made in size medium with about 95 yards of yarn.
Gauge and sizing: 9 stitches in 2 inches in Main Chart pattern. Finished neck measurement of 16.5 [18.5, 20.5] inches at the narrowest part.

Cast on: Cast on 148 [166, 184] stitches.

Body: To work the Main Chart, work columns 1-18 8 [9, 10] times, then work columns 19-22 once. Columns 19-22 are shaded to remind you to only work them once.

Work the Main Chart once. Row 1 and all odd rows are wrong-side rows (worked with the inside of the cowl facing you, following the wrong-side notations in the stitch key, and reading the chart from left to right). Row 2 and all even rows are right-side rows (worked with the outside of the cowl facing you, following the right-side notations in the stitch key, and reading the chart from right to left). 76 [85, 94] stitches remain.

Repeat rows 22-25 of the Main Chart until cowl reaches desired height. Stop after completing row 23 of the Main Chart.

Finishing: Cast off loosely. Weave in ends. Attach buttons on the edge opposite button holes. Block if desired.

Stitch Key

	RS: Knit WS: Purl
—	RS: Purl WS: Knit
◯	Yarn over
→	RS: Slip WS: Slip
/	Right leaning knit decrease
∠	Right leaning purl decrease

Main Chart

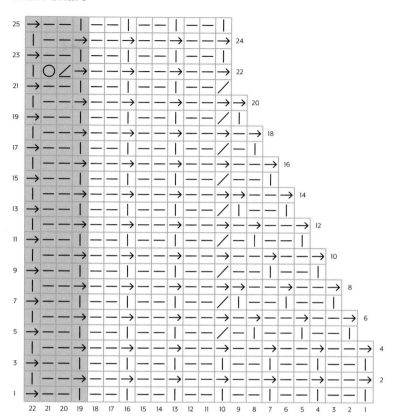

Chart notes: The shaded stitches are used to adjust sizing. To work the Main Chart, work columns 1-18 8 [9, 10] times, then work columns 19-22 once. Columns 19-22 are shaded to remind you to only work them once.

NARCISSUS PSEUDO-NARCISSUS

I am firmly convinced that daffodils are one of the best flowers for lazy gardeners like me (or perhaps I should say efficient gardeners). You drop dozens of them in the ground one cold fall day then forget about them all winter long. Come spring, you are rewarded with a sea of cheerful yellow. Best of all, they come back year after year. These projects are the same: a bit of work up front followed by lots of reward in the future. The socks draw on the rich greens and gentle curves of the leaves to produce an enchanting result. The cuffs echo the lovely flared shape of the flower itself. This is one of my favorite shapes for a cuff (it fits beautifully, keeps your hands warm, and doesn't get in the way of typing or knitting), and it's a perfect match for this image.

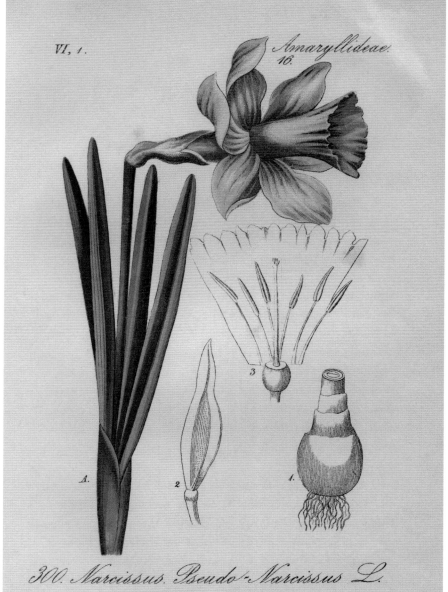

VI, 1.

Amaryllideae.
10.

A.

2

3

1.

300. *Narcissus Pseudo-Narcissus L.*
Unechte Narcisse.

NARCISSUS PSEUDO-NARCISSUS SOCK

Shown in: Adorn Sock by Three Irish Girls in the color Padraig. Made in size small with about 375 yards of yarn.
Gauge and sizing: 8 stitches in 1 inch in stockinette. Fits a foot or leg of about 8.5 [9.5] inches.
Notes: The heel flap directions are different for each size, be sure to follow the appropriate directions.

Cast on: Cast on 64 [72] stitches. Place marker and join for working in the round.

Cuff and leg: Throughout the sock, work only the unshaded columns for the smaller size, and work both the shaded and unshaded columns for the larger size. Work the appropriate Rib Chart 7 times. Work the appropriate Cuff Chart once. Work the appropriate Main Chart until sock reaches desired height. Stop after completing row 28 of the appropriate Main Chart.

Heel flap: The heel flap is worked over stitches 34-64 [38-72]. It uses a total of 31 [35] stitches.

Row 1 is a wrong-side row (worked with the inside of the sock facing you). Row 2 is a right-side row (worked with the outside of the sock facing you). Work these 2 rows 15 [17] times or until heel flap reaches desired length.

Small:
Row 1 (WS): Sl1, [ptbl1, k1] 15 times.
Row 2 (RS): Sl1, [ktbl1, p1] 15 times.

Large:
Row 1 (WS): Sl1, [k1, ptbl1] 17 times.
Row 2 (RS): Sl1, [p1, ktbl1] 17 times.

Heel turn: Odd rows are wrong-side rows (worked with the inside of the sock facing you). Even rows are right-side rows (worked with the outside of the sock facing you). Turn at the end of each row.

Row 1 (WS): Sl1, p17 [19], p2tog, p1.
Row 2 (RS): Sl1, k6, ssk, k1.
Row 3 (WS): Sl1, p7, p2tog, p1.
Row 4 (RS): Sl1, k8, ssk, k1.
Row 5 (WS): Sl1, p9, p2tog, p1.
Row 6 (RS): Sl1, k10, ssk, k1.
Row 7 (WS): Sl1, p11, p2tog, p1.
Row 8 (RS): Sl1, k12, ssk, k1.
Row 9 (WS): Sl1, p13, p2tog, p1.
Row 10 (RS): Sl1, k14, ssk, k1.
Row 11 (WS): Sl1, p15, p2tog, p1.
Row 12 (RS): Sl1, k16, ssk, k1.

Large, as above plus:
Row 13 (WS): Sl1, p17, p2tog, p1.
Row 14 (RS): Sl1, k18, ssk, k1.

19 [21] stitches remain.

Gusset and foot:
Setup round: Pick up and knit 1 stitch in each of the slipped stitches along the side of the heel flap, place first marker. Work across the top of the foot following the first row of the appropriate Main Chart for the first 32 [36] stitches, p the 33rd [37th] stitch, place second marker. Pick up and knit 1 stitch in each of the slipped stitches along the other side of the heel flap, k9 [10]. The round now begins in the middle of the bottom of the foot.

Decrease round: K until 3 stitches remain before first marker, k2tog, k1. Work across the top of the foot following the next row of the appropriate Main Chart for the first 32 [36] stitches, p the 33rd [37th] stitch. K1, ssk, k to end of round. 2 stitches decreased.

Non-decrease round: K to first marker. Work across the top of the foot following the next row of the appropriate Main Chart for the first 32 [36] stitches, p the 33rd [37th] stitch. K to end of round.

Alternate decrease and non-decrease rounds until 66 [74] stitches remain. Repeat the non-decrease round until you have worked the Main Chart once. Work the appropriate Toe Chart once. Repeat row 29 of the appropriate Toe Chart until sock measures 2 [2.75] inches shorter than desired length.

Toe:
Decrease round: K until 3 stitches remain before first marker, k2tog, k1. P1, ssp, p until 3 stitches remain before second marker, p2tog, p1. K1, ssk, k to end of round. 4 stitches decreased.

Non-decrease round: K to first marker. P to second marker. P to end of round.

Work these 2 rounds 6 [8] times, 42 stitches remain. Work the decrease round 6 more times, 18 stitches remain. K to marker. Remove markers. Graft toes. Weave in ends.

Stitch Key

ɫ Knit through the back loop

— Purl

O Yarn over

⟋ Right leaning twisted knit decrease

⟍ Left leaning twisted knit decrease

⋀ Centered twisted double knit decrease

Small Rib Chart

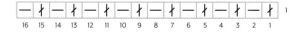

16 15 14 13 12 11 10 9 8 7 6 5 4 3 2 1

Large Rib Chart

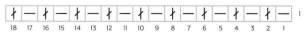

18 17 16 15 14 13 12 11 10 9 8 7 6 5 4 3 2 1

Chart notes: The left and right socks use different charts, be sure to follow the appropriate chart. The shaded stitches are used to adjust sizing. Throughout the sock, work only the unshaded columns for the smaller size, and work both the shaded and unshaded columns for the larger size.

Left Cuff Chart

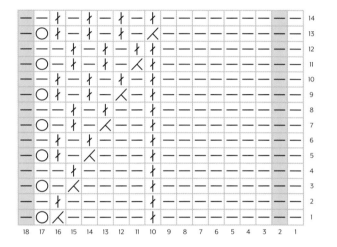

Right Cuff Chart

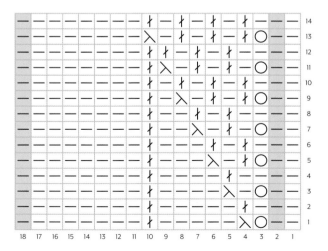

Left Main Chart

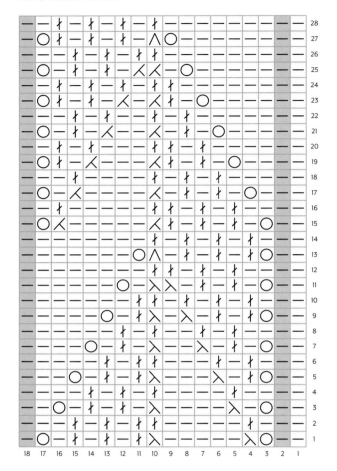

Left Toe Chart

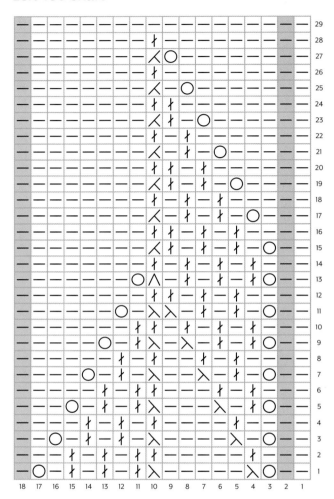

Right Main Chart

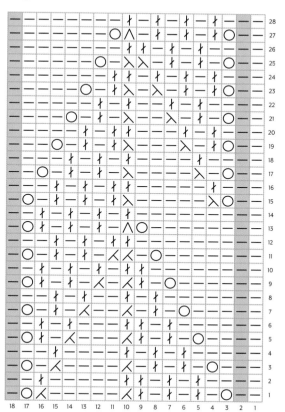

Right Toe Chart

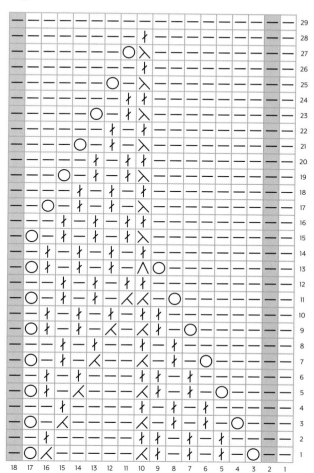

NARCISSUS PSEUDO-NARCISSUS CUFF

Shown in: Beckon Stretch Merino by Three Irish Girls in the color Burke. Made in size small with about 120 yards of yarn.
Gauge and sizing: 7 stitches in 1 inch in stockinette. Fits an arm of about 7 [8.75, 10.5] inches. Measure at the widest part of the arm that you want the cuff to cover.

Cast on: Cast on 72 [90, 108] stitches. Place marker and join for working in the round.

Hand and wrist: Work the Main Chart once. 48 [60, 72] stitches remain. Repeat rows 18 and 19 of the Main Chart until the cuff reaches desired length.

Finishing: Cast off loosely. Weave in ends. Block if desired.

BANDAGING —LEONARD.

Stitch Key

| | Knit

⟩ Knit through the back loop

— Purl

O Yarn over

→ Slip

⟨ Right leaning twisted knit decrease

⟩ Left leaning twisted knit decrease

⟋ Right leaning purl decrease

⟍ Left leaning purl decrease

Main Chart

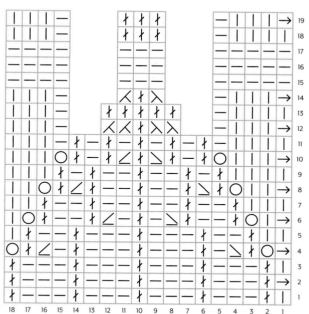

POLYPODIUM VULGARE

I love ferns, but I am absolutely terrible at growing my own. Despite a backyard that seems perfect for them, I've had no success at all. So I've had to content myself with including one here and hoping that someday I'll magically become a better gardener. In the meantime, these lovely, lacy socks just might be the perfect thing to console me. Their curved cuff and intricate texture remind me of curling fern fronds. The result is both beautiful and delicate. If you're looking for something a bit quicker and sturdier, this cowl might be just the ticket. It strips the idea of ferns down to the simplest interpretation. The resulting lace pattern is easy to work, and the cowl is both satisfyingly graphic and comfortingly substantial.

499.

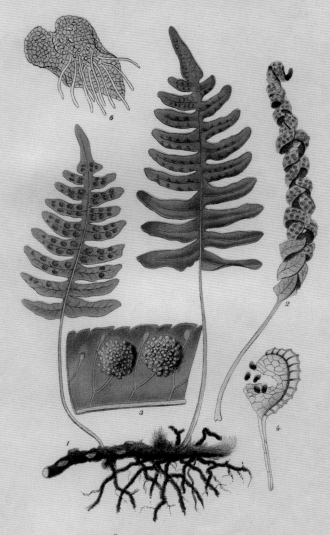

STENSÖTA, POLYPODIUM VULGARE L.

Gen. Stab. Lit. Anst.

POLYPODIUM VULGARE SOCK

Shown in: Tush by Saffron Dyeworks in the color New Growth. Made in size small with about 350 yards of yarn.
Gauge and sizing: 8 stitches in 1 inch in stockinette. Fits a foot or leg of about 8.5 [9.5] inches.

Cast on: Cast on 64 [72] stitches. Place marker and join for working in the round.

Cuff and leg: Throughout the sock, work only the unshaded columns for the smaller size and work both the shaded and unshaded columns for the larger size. Work the Main Chart until sock reaches desired height. Stop after completing row 16 of the Main Chart.

Heel flap: The heel flap is worked over stitches 34-64 [38-72]. It uses 31 [35] stitches.

Row 1 is a wrong-side row (worked with the inside of the sock facing you). Row 2 is a right-side row (worked with the outside of the sock facing you). Work these 2 rows 15 [17] times or until heel flap reaches desired length.

Row 1 (WS): (Sl1, p1) 15 [17] times, k1.
Row 2 (RS): Sl1, (k1, p1) 15 [17] times.

Heel turn: Odd rows are wrong-side rows (worked with the inside of the sock facing you). Even rows are right-side rows (worked with the outside of the sock facing you). Turn at the end of each row.

Row 1 (WS): Sl1, p17 [19], p2tog, p1.
Row 2 (RS): Sl1, k6, ssk, k1.
Row 3 (WS): Sl1, p7, p2tog, p1.
Row 4 (RS): Sl1, k8, ssk, k1.

Row 5 (WS): Sl1, p9, p2tog, p1.
Row 6 (RS): Sl1, k10, ssk, k1.
Row 7 (WS): Sl1, p11, p2tog, p1.
Row 8 (RS): Sl1, k12, ssk, k1.
Row 9 (WS): Sl1, p13, p2tog, p1.
Row 10 (RS): Sl1, k14, ssk, k1.
Row 11 (WS): Sl1, p15, p2tog, p1.
Row 12 (RS): Sl1, k16, ssk, k1.

Large, as above plus:
Row 13 (WS): Sl1, p17, p2tog, p1.
Row 14 (RS): Sl1, k18, ssk, k1.

19 [21] stitches remain.

Gusset and foot:
Setup round: Pick up and knit stitches along the side of the heel flap, place first marker. Work across the top of the foot following the first row of the Main Chart for the first 32 [36] stitches, k the 33rd [37th] stitch, place second marker. Pick up and knit stitches along the other side of the heel flap, k9 [10]. The round now begins in the middle of the bottom of the foot.

Decrease round: K until 3 stitches remain before first marker, k2tog, k1. Work across the top of the foot following the next row of the Main Chart for the first 32 [36] stitches, k the 33rd [37th] stitch. K1, ssk, k to end of round. 2 stitches decreased.

Non-decrease round: K to first marker. Work across the top of the foot following the next row of the Main Chart for the first 32 [36] stitches, k the 33rd [37th] stitch. K to end of round.

Alternate decrease and non-decrease rounds until 66 [74] stitches remain. Repeat the non-decrease round until you have worked 2 repeats of the Main Chart. Begin working the Main Chart once more. Stop after completing row 10 of the Main Chart. Work the Toe Chart once. Repeat row 7 of the Toe Chart until sock measures 2 [2.75] inches shorter than desired length.

Toe:
Decrease round: K until 3 stitches remain before first marker, k2tog, k1. K1, ssk, k until 3 stitches remain before second marker, k2tog, k1. K1, ssk, k to end of round. 4 stitches decreased.

Non-decrease round: K to end of round.

Work these 2 rounds 6 [8] times, 42 stitches remain. Work the decrease round 6 more times, 18 stitches remain. K to marker. Remove markers. Graft toes. Weave in ends.

Stitch Key

| | Knit

⊁ Knit through the back loop

O Yarn over

/ Right leaning knit decrease

\ Left leaning knit decrease

 Right leaning double knit decrease

 Left leaning double knit decrease

 Centered double knit decrease

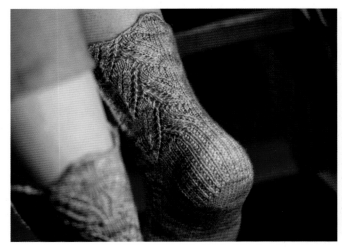

Main Chart

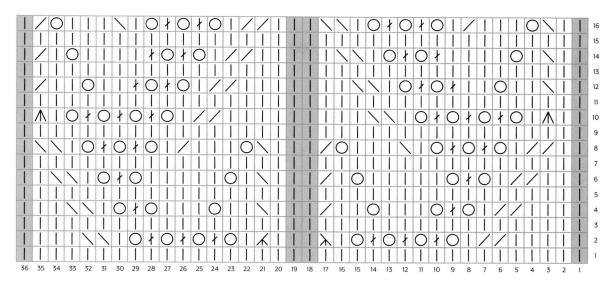

Toe Chart

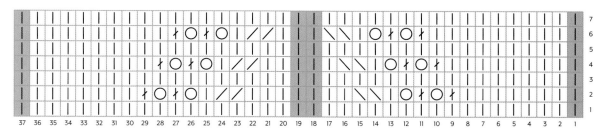

Chart notes: The shaded stitches are used to adjust sizing. Throughout the sock, work only the unshaded columns for the smaller size and work both the shaded and unshaded columns for the larger size.

POLYPODIUM VULGARE COWL

Shown in: Mica by Saffron Dyeworks in the color Botanical. Made in the 112-stitch size with about 200 yards of yarn.
Gauge and sizing: 16 stitches in 3 inches in stockinette. Finished circumference of 18.5 [21.5, 24.5, 27.5] inches.

Cast on: Cast on 96 [112, 128, 144] stitches. Place marker and join for working in the round.

Body: Work 3 rounds of k. Work the Main Chart until cowl reaches desired height. Stop after completing row 14 or row 28 of the Main Chart. Work 3 rounds of k.

Finishing: Cast off loosely, weave in ends. Block if desired.

Stitch Key

| | Knit

ⴕ Knit through the back loop

◯ Yarn over

╱ Right leaning knit decrease

╲ Left leaning knit decrease

Main Chart

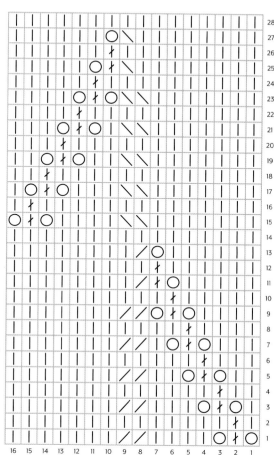

LOASA LATERITIA

These are probably one of the less well-known plants featured in this collection, but they were just too lovely not to include even if they were a bit unfamiliar. Their strikingly angular orange petals drew my attention immediately. I echoed their shape for the pattern on the sock's cuff. The folded over edges of the petals seemed a perfect excuse to do a sock with a turned-down cuff. The result is utterly charming. The delicate green color and strong diagonal lines of the lovely little spiral thing (I think it's a seed pod, but I'm ashamed to admit I don't know for sure) inspired the cowl. It's marvelously simple to knit. It may actually be the easiest project in the whole book, but the end result is terribly impressive.

LOASA LATERITIA

Nat. size

PL. 109

LOASA LATERITIA SOCK

Shown in: Rune by Barking Dog Yarns in the color Paprika. Made in size medium with about 325 yards of yarn.
Gauge and sizing: 8 stitches in 1 inch in stockinette. Fits a foot or leg of about 7.5 [8.5, 9.5] inches.

Cast on: Using needles 1 size bigger than those needed to get gauge, cast on 56 [64, 72] stitches. Place marker and join for working in the round.

Cuff and leg: Using needles 1 size bigger than those needed to get gauge, work the Main Chart once. Switch to smaller needles.

Turn the cuff. To do this, wrap the yarn around the next stitch. To do this, bring the yarn to the front, slip the first stitch of the next round to the right needle, bring the yarn to the back, slip the same stitch back to the left needle.

The next step is to turn the cuff inside out (along the purl ridge) so that the inside of the cuff pattern is facing out. This ensures that the outside of the cuff pattern will show when the cuff is turned down when the sock is worn.

The final step is to place a marker to indicate the start of the round.

Work 50 rows of p1, k3 ribbing.

Heel flap: The heel flap is worked over stitches 30-56 [34-64, 38-72]. It uses 27 [31, 35] stitches.

Row 1 is a wrong-side row (worked with the inside of the sock facing you). Row 2 is a right-side row (worked with the outside of the

sock facing you). Work these 2 rows 13 [15, 17] times or until heel flap reaches desired length.

Row 1 (WS): Sl1, p2, (k1, p1, sl1, p1) 5 [6, 7] times, k1, p3.
Row 2 (RS): Sl1, k2, (p1, k3) 6 [7, 8] times.

Heel turn: Odd rows are wrong-side rows (worked with the inside of the sock facing you). Even rows are right-side rows (worked with the outside of the sock facing you). Turn at the end of each row.

Row 1 (WS): Sl1, p15 [17, 19], p2tog, p1.
Row 2 (RS): Sl1, k6, ssk, k1.
Row 3 (WS): Sl1, p7, p2tog, p1.
Row 4 (RS): Sl1, k8, ssk, k1.
Row 5 (WS): Sl1, p9, p2tog, p1.
Row 6 (RS): Sl1, k10, ssk, k1.
Row 7 (WS): Sl1, p11, p2tog, p1.
Row 8 (RS): Sl1, k12, ssk, k1.
Row 9 (WS): Sl1, p13, p2tog, p1.
Row 10 (RS): Sl1, k14, ssk, k1.

Medium and large, as above plus:
Row 11 (WS): Sl1, p15, p2tog, p1.
Row 12 (RS): Sl1, k16, ssk, k1.

Large, as above plus:
Row 13 (WS): Sl1, p17, p2tog, p1.
Row 14 (RS): Sl1, k18, ssk, k1.

17 [19, 21] stitches remain.

Gusset and foot:
Setup round: Pick up and knit 1 stitch in each of the slipped stitches along the side of the heel flap, place first marker. Work across the top of the foot continuing the p1, k3 ribbing as established, beginning and ending with a p, place second marker. Pick up and knit 1 stitch in each of the slipped stitches along the other side of the heel flap, k8 [9, 10]. The round now begins in the middle of the bottom of the foot.

Decrease round: K until 3 stitches remain before first marker, k2tog, k1. Work across the top of the foot continuing the ribbing as established. K1, ssk, k to end of round. 2 stitches decreased.

Non-decrease round: K to first marker. Work across the top of the foot continuing the ribbing as established. K to end of round.

Alternate decrease and non-decrease rounds until 58 [66, 74] stitches remain. Repeat the non-decrease round until sock measures 1.5 [1.75, 2] inches shorter than desired length.

Toe:
Decrease round: K until 3 stitches remain before first marker, k2tog, k1. P1, ssk, follow ribbing as established until 3 stitches remain before second marker, k2tog, p1. K1, ssk, k to end of round. 4 stitches decreased.

Non-decrease round: K to first marker. Follow ribbing as established to second marker. K to end of round.

Work these 2 rounds 4 [6, 8] times, 42 stitches remain. Work the decrease round 6 more times, 18 stitches remain. K to marker. Remove markers. Graft toes. Weave in ends.

Stitch Key

| Knit

⅄ Knit through the back loop

— Purl

◯ Yarn over

╱ Right leaning twisted knit decrease

╲ Left leaning twisted knit decrease

⋀ Centered double knit decrease

Main Chart

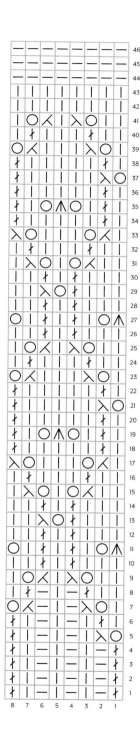

Chart notes: When a centered double decrease is the first stitch on the needle, it requires extra attention. The double decrease
turns 3 stitches into 1. When the double decrease happens at the beginning of a needle,
the first of those 3 stitches is the last stitch of
the previous needle.

For example, the first stitch of round 11 of the
Main Chart is a centered double decrease. The
decrease will use the last stitch of round 10
and the first 2 stitches of round 11. To make the
decrease, do not work the last stitch of round
10. Instead, use it as the first of the 3 stitches
of the decrease as described in the stitch key.
The completed stitch will be the first stitch of
round 11.

LOASA LATERITIA COWL

Shown in: Etheria by Barking Dog Yarns in the color Rock Moss. Made in size medium with about 300 yards of yarn.
Gauge and sizing: 5 stitches in 1 inch in Main Chart pattern. Finished circumference of 20 [30, 40] inches.

Cast on: Cast on 100 [150, 200] stitches. Place marker and join for working in the round.

Body: Work 3 rounds of k. Repeat the Main Chart until cowl reaches desired height, always moving the beginning of round marker back 1 stitch at the end of round 2. That is, follow row 2 of the Main Chart until 1 stitch remains in the round. Move your start of round marker so that this 1 remaining stitch becomes the first stitch of the next round. Now start following row 1 of the Main Chart. Once cowl reaches desired height, work 3 rounds of k.

Finishing: Bind off loosely. Weave in ends. Block if desired.

Stitch Key

| | Knit

− Purl

○ Yarn over

∩ Slip forward

∕ Right leaning purl decrease

Chart notes: The start point of the chart changes. I recommend using a stitch marker even if you usually don't use them.

Main Chart

LINARIA BIPARTITA

The instant I saw the name purple toadflax, I was hopelessly smitten. How could I possibly resist a name like that? The lovely images were just a bonus at that point. I knew a plant like this demanded a bit of drama. For the socks, I found that drama in repetition. A simple, sharply pointed petal shape tiled seamlessly across the body of the sock with just a bit of complimentary ribbing at the heel and toe looked absolutely smashing. For the shawl, the drama comes from both the size of the project and from the design. I won't deny it, this shawl is a big undertaking, but it's fairly simple as shawls go. All the fancy stitchwork happens along the spine while the rest of it is soothingly simple. The end result is more than worth the work.

PURPLE TOADFLAX

(LINARIA BIPARTITA)

Nat. size

PL. 207

LINARIA BIPARTITA SOCK

Shown in: Piquant Lite by Hazel Knits in the color Chocoberry. Made in size medium with about 300 yards of yarn.
Gauge and sizing: 8 stitches in 1 inch in stockinette. Fits a foot or leg of about 7.5 [8.5, 9.5] inches.
Notes: The heel flap directions are different for each size, be sure to follow the appropriate directions.

Cast on: Cast on 56 [64, 72] stitches. Place marker and join for working in the round.

Cuff and leg: Work the Cuff Chart 8 times. Work the Main Chart until sock reaches desired height. Stop after completing row 16 of the Main Chart. For the smallest and largest sizes, start following the Cuff Chart and Main Chart at column 2 instead of at column 1.

Heel flap: The heel flap is worked over stitches 31-56 [33-64, 39-72]. It uses a total of 26 [32, 34] stitches.

Row 1 is a wrong-side row (worked with the inside of the sock facing you). Row 2 is a right-side row (worked with the outside of the sock facing you). Work these 2 rows 13 [16, 17] times or until heel flap reaches desired length.

Medium:
Row 1 (WS): (Sl1, k1, p1, k2, p1, k1, sl1) 3 times, sl1, k1, p1, k2, p1, k2.
Row 2 (RS): Sl1, p1, k1, p2, k1, p2, (p2, k1, p2, k1, p2) 3 times.

Small and Large:
Row 1 (WS): Sl1, k1, (k1, p1, k2, p1, k1, sl2) 2 [–, 3] times, k1, p1, k2, p1, k3.
Row 2 (RS): Sl1, p1, (p1, k1, p2, k1, p3), 3 [–, 4] times.

Heel turn: Odd rows are wrong-side rows (worked with the inside of the sock facing you). Even rows are right-side rows (worked with the outside of the sock facing you). Turn at the end of each row.

Row 1 (WS): Sl1, p14 [18, 18], p2tog, p1.
Row 2 (RS): Sl1, k5 [7, 5], ssk, k1.
Row 3 (WS): Sl1, p6 [8, 6], p2tog, p1.
Row 4 (RS): Sl1, k7 [9, 7], ssk, k1.
Row 5 (WS): Sl1, p8 [10, 8], p2tog, p1.
Row 6 (RS): Sl1, k9 [11, 9], ssk, k1.
Row 7 (WS): Sl1, p10 [12, 10], p2tog, p1.
Row 8 (RS): Sl1, k11 [13, 11], ssk, k1.
Row 9 (WS): Sl1, p12 [14, 12], p2tog, p1.
Row 10 (RS): Sl1, k13 [15, 13], ssk, k1.

Medium and Large, as above plus:
Row 11 (WS): Sl1, p—[16, 14], p2tog, p1.
Row 12 (RS): Sl1, k—[17, 15], ssk, k1.

Large, as above plus:
Row 13 (WS): Sl1, p—[—, 16], p2tog, p1.
Row 14 (RS): Sl1, k—[—, 17], ssk, k1.

16 [20, 20] stitches remain.

Gusset and foot:
Setup round: Pick up and knit 1 stitch in each of the slipped stitches along the side of the heel flap, place first marker. Work across the top of the foot following the first row of the Main Chart, place second marker. Pick up and knit 1 stitch in each of the slipped stitches along the other side of the heel flap, k8 [10, 10]. The round now begins in the middle of the bottom of the foot. As on the leg, for the smallest and largest sock, start following the Main Chart at column 2 instead of at column 1.

Decrease round: K until 3 stitches remain before first marker, k2tog, k1. Work across the top of the foot following the next row of the Main Chart. K1, ssk, k to end of round. 2 stitches decreased.

Non-decrease round: K to first marker. Work across the top of the foot following the next row of the Main Chart. K to end of round.

Alternate decrease and non-decrease rounds until 60 [64, 76] stitches remain. Repeat the non-decrease round until sock measures 3 inches shorter than desired length. Stop after completing row 16 of the Main Chart. Repeat row 16 of the Main Chart until sock measures 1.5 [1.75, 2] inches shorter than desired length.

Toe:
Decrease round: K until 3 stitches remain before first marker, k1. P1 [2, 1], ssk, follow ribbing as established by row 16 of the Main Chart until 3 [4, 3] stitches remain before second marker, k2tog, p1 [2, 1]. K1, ssk, k to end of round. 4 stitches decreased.

Non-decrease round: K to first marker. Follow ribbing as established by row 16 of the Main Chart to second marker. K to end of round.

Work these 2 rounds 4 [5, 8] times, 44 stitches remain. Work the decrease round 7 more times, 16 stitches remain. K to marker. Remove markers. Graft toes. Weave in ends.

Stitch Key

| Knit

— Purl

O Yarn over

/ Right leaning knit decrease

\ Left leaning knit decrease

|∧| 1 by 1 Cable variable

Cuff Chart

| — | — | │ | │ | — | — | │ | — | — | 1 |
| 8 | 7 | 6 | 5 | 4 | 3 | 2 | 1 |

Main Chart

Chart rows 1–16, columns 8 7 6 5 4 3 2 1

Chart notes: The smallest and largest sizes start following the chart at an unusual point (column 2 instead of at column 1).

The first stitch of row 5 of the Main Chart is a cable. This cable is worked with the last stitch of round 4 and the first stitch of round 5. These 2 stitches are crossed over each other as you work the cable. Be sure to pay attention to this as you reach the end of round 4.

For size medium, when working the foot, row 5 of the Main Chart will both begin and end with a cable. That is, the last stitch of the gusset and the first stitch of the top of the foot will cross each other. The last stitch of the top of the foot and the first stitch of the gusset will also cross each other. You will work a total of 5 cables as you work row 5.

LINARIA BIPARTITA SHAWL

Designed with the help of Elizabeth Inman.

Shown in: DK Lively by Hazel Knits in the color Cotton Candy. Made with the Body Chart worked 4 times with about 800 yards of yarn.
Gauge and sizing: 5.75 stitches in 1 inch in stockinette. The shawl as shown is about 7 feet across at the top.
Notes: The first 3 and last 3 stitches of every row are always knit. Each right-side row except the very last one increases the total stitch count by 4. The very last one increases the total stitch count by 2.

Cast on: Cast on 3 stitches.

Set up: K 6 rows. Turn work 90 degrees clockwise (live stitches are on the right, working yarn is on the top). Pick up and knit 3 stitches (6 stitches on the needle). Turn work 90 degrees clockwise (live stitches are on the right, working yarn is on the top). Pick up and knit 3 stitches in the cast on edge (9 stitches on the needle). K3, p3, k3.

Charted sections: Note that the Point Chart, Body Chart, and End Chart show only the right-side rows. On wrong-side rows, k3, p until 3 stitches remain, k3.

Work the Point Chart once (93 stitches on the needle).

Work the Body Chart once. The first time you work it, work the 12 shaded stitches on each side of the chart twice. If you work the Body Chart a second time, work the 12 shaded stitches on each side of the chart 4 times. Continue in this fashion, working the 12 shaded stitches on each side of the chart an extra 2 times each time you work the Body Chart, until the piece reaches desired size. Stop after completing row 24 of the Body Chart. 48 stitches increased with each repeat of the Body Chart.

Work the End Chart once. When you work the End Chart, work the 12 shaded stitches on each side of the chart 2 more times than you did on the final repeat of the Body Chart. Stop after completing row 11 of the End Chart. 24 stitches increased.

The Edge Chart shows both right-side rows and wrong-side rows. Row 1 is a wrong-side row (worked with the inside of the shawl facing you, following the wrong-side notations in the stitch key, and reading the chart from left to right). Row 2 is a right-side row (worked with the outside of the shawl facing you, following the right-side notations in the stitch key, and reading the chart from right to left) Work the Edge Chart once. When you work the Edge Chart, repeat the 12 shaded stitches on each side of the chart 1 more time than you did on the End Chart. 2 stitches increased.

Finishing: Cast off as follows, k1, (yo, k1, put left needle into 2 right-most stitches on the right needle and pull both over the stitch that was just knit and off the needle), repeat to end. Weave in ends. Block if desired.

Chart notes: The Point Chart, Body Chart, and End Chart show only the right-side rows. On wrong-side rows, k3, p until 3 stitches remain, k3.

The shaded stitches in the Body Chart, End Chart, and Edge Chart are used to adjust sizing. Pay close attention to the instructions.

The charts are large and have been broken across two pages to make them easier to read. The center stitch is outlined in red and repeated on each page to help orient you. Be sure to only work this center stitch once.

Stitch Key

|	Knit
—	RS: Purl / WS: Knit
O	Yarn over
/	Right leaning knit decrease
\	Left leaning knit decrease
∧	Centered double decrease
Ƙ	Make 1 right knitwise
Y	Make 1 left knitwise
☐	Center Stitch

Edge Left

Columns: 71 70 69 68 67 66 65 64 63 62 61 60 59 58 57 56 55 54 53 52 51 50 49 48 47 46 45 44 43 42 41 40 39 38 37 36

Row 3: — — — (knit/purl row)
Row 2: | | | O/O/O/O/O I O/O/O/O∧O/O/O/O I O/O/O/O/O∧
Row 1: — — — (knit/purl row)

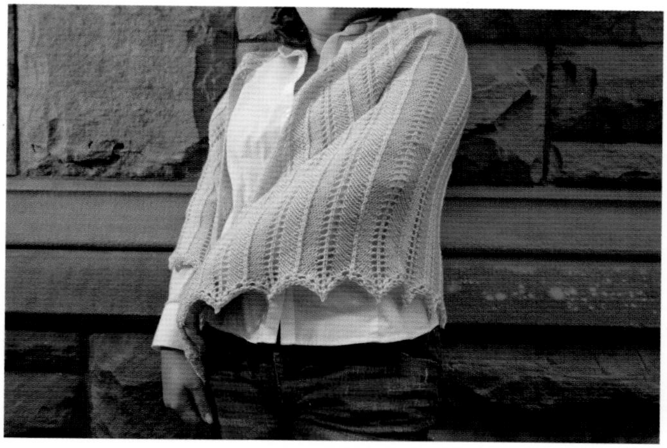

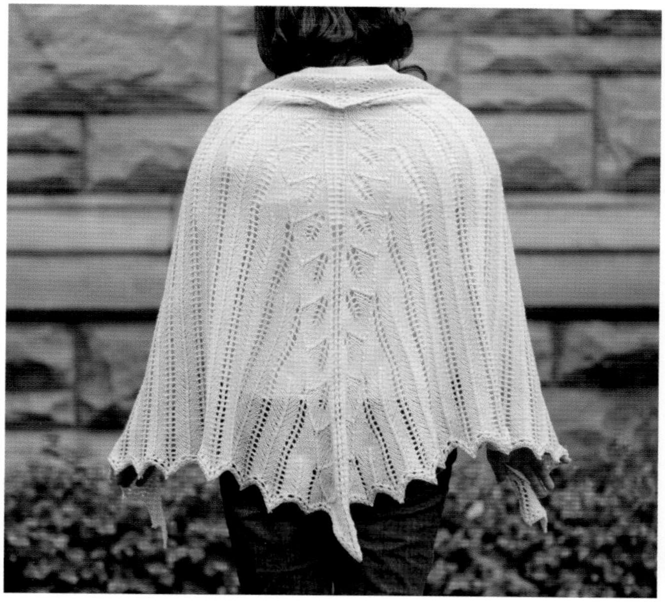

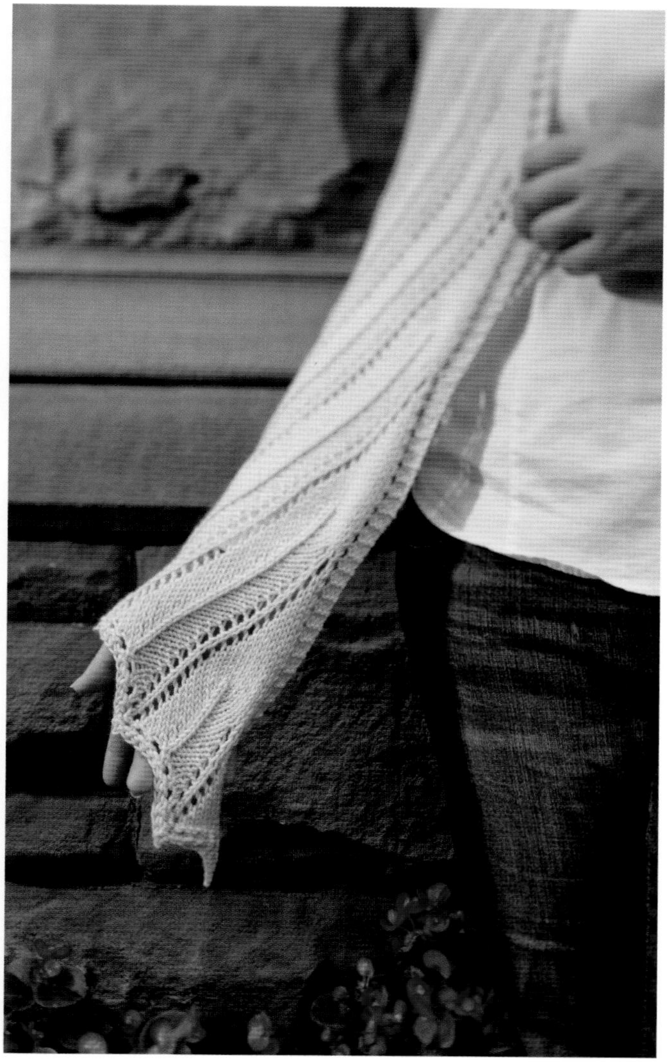

Edge Right

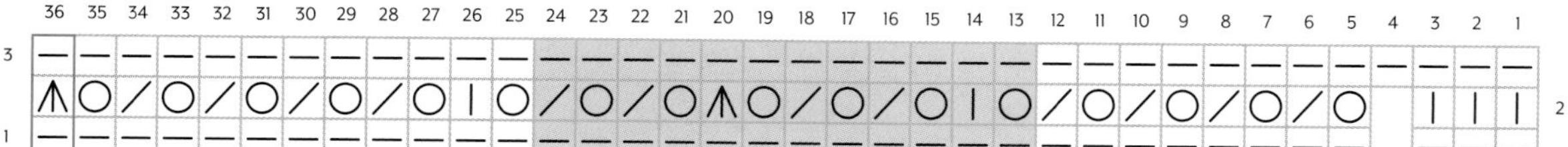

End Left

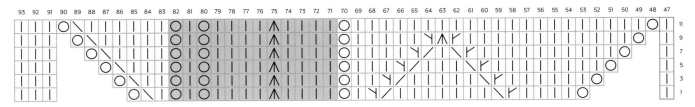

Body Left

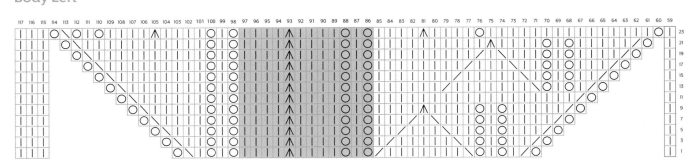

Point Left

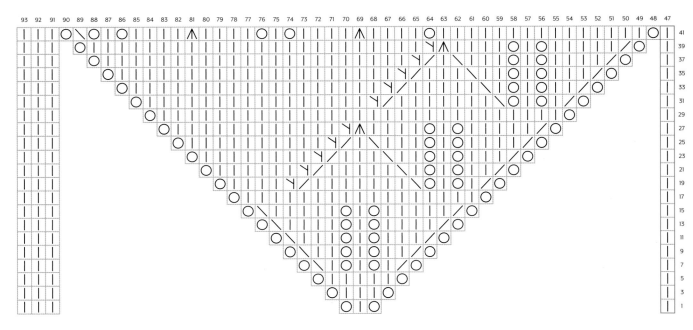

End Right

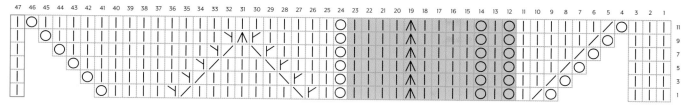

Body Right

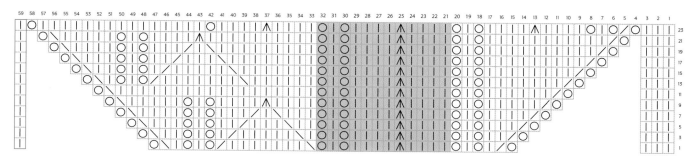

Point Right

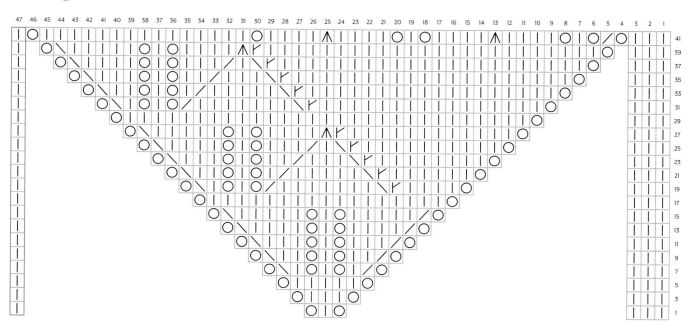

SOURCES

Crocus vernus projects use Handwerks Textiles yarns—handwerkstextiles.com. The socks are made with Sock Plus 8 (396 yards per skein) in Misty Morning. The mitts are made with So-Soft DK (230 yards per skein) in Lemongrass.

Chrysanthemum frutescens projects use Sanguine Gryphon yarns, now Verdant Gryphon and Cephalopod Yarns—verdantgryphon.com, cephalopodyarns.com. The socks are made with Bugga! (412 yards per skein) in Oleander Nymph. The hat is made with Traveller (280 yards per skein) in Ireland.

Rubus suberectus projects use Blue Moon Fiber Arts yarns—bluemoonfiberarts.com. The socks are made with Socks that Rock Mediumweight (380 yards per skein) in Ghillie Dhu. The shawl is made with Woobu (620 yards per skein) in Jasper. The shawl pin is from karismabykara.com.

Pinus silvestris projects use Sweet Georgia yarns—sweetgeorgiayarns.com. The socks are made with Silk Crush (375 yards per skein) in Deep Olive. The hat is made with Merino Silk Aran (185 yards per skein) in Cayenne.

Rosa rubiginosa projects use Sundara Yarns—sundarayarn.com. The socks are made with Sock (370 yards per skein) in Dahlia. The mitts are made with DK Silky Cashmere (160 yards per skein) in Black Cherry.

Dianthus superbus projects use The Schaefer Yarn Company yarns—schaeferyarn.com. The socks are made with Nichole (405 yards per skein) in Thistle. The cowl is made with Chris (215 yards per skein) in Pomegranate.

Narcissus pseudo-narcissus projects use Three Irish Girls yarns—threeirishgirls.com. The socks are made with Adorn Sock (430 yards per skein) in Padraig. The cuffs are made with Beckon Stretch Merino (370 yards per skein) in Burke.

Polypodium vulgare projects use Saffron Dyeworks yarns—saffrondyeworks.com. The socks are made with Tush (440 yards per skein) in New Growth. The cowl is made with Mica (230 yards per skein) in Botanical.

Loasa lateritia projects use Barking Dog Yarns—barkingdogyarns.com. The socks are made with Rune (435 yards per skein) in Paprika. The cowl is made with Etheria (340 yards per skein) in Rock Moss.

Linaria bipartita projects use Hazel Knits yarns—hazelknits.com. The socks are made with Piquant Lite (400 yards per skein) in Chocoberry. The shawl is made with DK Lively (275 yards per skein) in Cotton Candy.

All charts created with StitchMastery Knitting Chart Editor—stitchmastery.com.

All photographs were taken by Brett Yacovella of Making the Moment—makingthemoment.com.

Book and cover design by Zoë Lonergan—zoelonergan.com.